PRAISE FROM PARENTS

After reading her blog, *Parents of Grown Offspring (POGO)*, subscribers had this to say:

"Thank you for your blog, Barbara. My children are wonderful, loving 40-something adults, but parenting instincts persist and complicate matters when not held in check, and our feelings can be hurt when our advice isn't appreciated. Having you and your psychological experts address this complicated part of our lives in detail is invaluable." A.L.

"Barbara, you have a real winner here. Great idea to help parents with all the myriad "situations" that come up with adult offspring. POGO is filling the void in such an important area, especially in our present environment." S.P.

"Thank you for allowing me in your community." R.L.

"I so enjoy POGO. It fills a need that is often not met, specifically, to receive sound insights, approaches, and advice for our age segment and, equally, to express one's stance on important family issues. I find most valuable the topics of money (in all its manifestations), grandchild rearing, and lifestyle." P.D.

"Terrific! I look forward to every issue." H.C.

"Thanks for posting such informative articles with lots of positive reinforcement! It's always helpful to get others' perspective on your many important topics." H.B .

"Barbara, I'm in awe of your posts. Using the literature sources that are out there and on-line is a brilliant solution to this obvious need. Keep on keeping on." D.B.

"You are working hard to make us folks with grown children necessary." A.R.

"Thank you for your blog. It is so reassuring, not only in terms of offspring, but also siblings who we had trouble relating to or living with. It seems so appropriate to blame ourselves, but knowing there is concrete evidence that so much is genetic is comforting." G.Y.

"I always enjoy POGO's incidents/insights—so authentic, capturing a broad range of experiences." D.P.

"Very helpful!" C.G.

"Barbara, you are spot on!" S.G.

"POGO is fulling a real niche. Some people really think outside the box. You're one." G.B.

"Love your articles and upbeat attitude." S.S.

"Another winner, Barbara. Thanks for sending." J.M.

"I think this is great! Congrats! I'm sure you won't mind if I share this with a few of my friends! M.R.

"CONGRATULATIONS, Barbara! This is a beautiful and informative presentation. I look forward to it every Tuesday and to being a POGO subscriber! You must be so proud. POGO is a WINNER!!!" J.G.

"Wonderful, Barbara! I will share this with my friends." L.H.

"Your articles on the transfer of money and the need for wills are so important. I'm forwarding them on to my grown children, who need to do some estate planning for their children." J.S.

"Congratulations! This is such a beautiful blog and so well thought-out… everything is tip-top. I will be reading along and thinking of you…never content to sit on your back porch, sipping Margaritas…" A.C.

Parents of Adult Children

BOOKS BY BARBARA GREENLEAF

Parents of Adult Children: You are Not Alone

THIS OLD BODY: And 99 Other Reasons to Laugh at Life

HELP: A Handbook for Working Mothers
with Lewis A. Schaffer, M.D.

Children Through the Ages: A History of Childhood

America Fever: The Story of American Immigration

Young Adult Novels

Good-to-Go Café
Animal Kingdom

Juvenile Biography

Forward March to Freedom:
A Biography of A. Philip Randolph

PARENTS OF ADULT CHILDREN
You Are Not Alone

BARBARA GREENLEAF

More Mesa Press

Published by
More Mesa Press
Post Office Box 610
Goleta, CA 93116

ISBN paperback: 978-1-5136-5904-6
ISBN (ebook): 978-1-5136-5905-3

Library of Congress Control Number: 2020900695
For information, group sales, and booking Barbara
for your next event:
Barbara@barbaragreenleaf.com

Barbara Greenleaf makes no claims to being a therapist. Neither her advice nor that of any of the parents and experts contributing to this book is intended to replace guidance from licensed professionals.

For reprint permission, grateful acknowledgment is made to:

Jeffrey Bernstein, Ph.D.: "5 Signs of Manipulation," and "3 Ways to Get Closer to Your Adult Child."

Marianne Bohr: "Saying Goodbye," by Marianne Bohr.

Deanna Brann, PhD: "How Not to Sweat the Small Stuff with your Daughter-in-Law."

Phyllis Cohen: "Leave a Legacy of . . . Interesting."

Donne Davis: "Learning the Boundaries of Communication," "What Mothers-in-Law Wish they could tell their Daughters-in-Law," and "The Double-Edged Nature of Being a Grandma."

Terry Haward: "A Mother's Regret: When Grown Siblings Don't Get Along."

Laura Kenig: "Losing Zane."

Deborah Levinson: "Losing a Husband/Losing a Father."

Pamela Reynolds: "5 Ways to Deal with Uneasy Mother/Daughter-in-Law Moments" and "How to Communicate with Distant and Uncommunicative In-Laws."

Lori R. Sackler: "How to Talk to your Adult Kids about their Inheritance."

Linda Schwartz: "Standing on the Shore," "My Father's Hands," "Flowers and Empathy," "Shadow Box of the Heart," and "The Circle of Life."

To Jon, Always

Contents

3
Mothers and Daughters, Fathers and Sons

4
The Generation Gap

5
The Fractured Family

6
Staying In Touch With Your Feelings and Each Other

7
Special Situations

8
Leaving a Legacy

Preface

*"No mother is ever, completely, a child's idea
of what a mother should be, and I suppose it
works the other way around as well. But despite
everything, we didn't do too badly by one
another, we did as well as most."*
Margaret Atwood, *The Handmaid's Tale*

While parents of young children have tons of information and advice at their disposal, there's very little out there for parents of adult children. This is surprising because our grown children will be with us three times as long as when they were young. Moreover, our interactions with adult children are much more complex. Even so, many parents don't get the information they could use by discussing vexing issues with friends. There's still pressure in our society to pretend, perhaps even to ourselves, that everything is perfect with the kids. After all, aren't our grown children life's report card? And everyone wants to get an A in parenting. In January of 2017 when I started my blog, *Parents of Grown Offspring (POGO)*, on which this book is based, I wanted to enlighten and liberate mothers and fathers from the code of silence. I sought to:

- Let parents know they're not the only ones.

- Provide constructive advice from experts and personal testimony from peers.

- Stimulate thinking and discussion about parent-adult child relationships.

I have long been interested in the family both as a historian and a journalist. Years before I started POGO, I authored *Children Through the Ages: A History of Childhood* and *HELP: A Handbook for Working Mothers* with Lewis Schaffer, M.D., as well as numerous articles for *Working Mother* magazine. I've also written books for children and young adults, having started in the book and education department at *The New York Times*. Finally, as the mother of two and grandmother of four, I can use the pronoun "we" legitimately!

In my research for this book, I found that while most of the older generation takes the fourth commandment, "Honor thy mother and father," quite literally, the younger generation puts a different and much more casual spin on it. We showed up for Sunday dinner, gave presents on milestone occasions, and sent cards on Mother's Day. They often think that's corny and don't feel it's up to them to create family togetherness. It is this disconnect between the parents' expectations and the younger generation's sense of obligation that seems to cause the most friction, with many parents feeling underappreciated and their adult offspring feeling put upon. This book shows the way forward.

Method and Structure

In the past three years I interviewed dozens of parents and adult children for POGO. I found that if they were to share openly, I had to offer them anonymity, which is understandable given the sensitive nature of their personal stories. Thus, most of the interviewees are identified only with a first name and last initial. The professionals are cited by their real names.

There are three components to the book:

- Articles: I wrote most of the blog posts myself, but I also included guest contributors with special expertise or perspectives.

- "Think about It" scenarios: Throughout the book I feature thorny adult family situations and a panel's opinions on how the parents should handle them.

- Readers' comments and poems. Finally, I include some representative reader views and poems that touch the heart in a way that prose cannot.

If there's one thing I learned in the course of all my research, it is that there's no one ideal American family. I've included families for whom parent-adult child relationships are working fine as well as those who are struggling. No matter where you fall on the continuum, I hope you will feel this book lives up to its subtitle, "You are not alone." *Parents of Adult Children* is with you every step of the way to the brave, new world of the adult family. Thank you for coming along for the ride.

Chapter 1

The Difficult Daughter-in-Law

I am starting out this book with articles about the difficult daughter-in-law (DDIL) because there's so much interest in and angst about her. My blog pieces obviously hit a nerve because parents searched my DDIL articles on the Internet six times more than all my other posts combined! The mother-in-law (MIL) may be the source of jokes, but the DDIL is the source of heartache in many American homes. Here's the gist of the avalanche of comments I received on this fraught topic:

- Our daughter-in-law's cruel treatment of us is unbelievable and impossible to understand.
- She's turned our son against us, and now she's turning our grandchildren against us, too.
- Our son only calls when he's alone.
- He believes all her lies.
- She won't let me see my grandchildren.
- Her mother is also manipulative and spiteful.
- She comes from a dysfunctional family and is equally aggressive toward me.
- She sees every relationship as a power struggle.
- Our daughter-in-law is a narcissist.
- She won't speak to me.

- She won't say what we did wrong.
- She's the nastiest person I know.
- She only lets me see her children if I'm supervised.
- She treats her family totally differently, and that's where she and my son spend every holiday.
- For some reason daughters-in-law are much more problematical than sons-in-law.
- I thought she'd come around, but it's been a decade and there's still no communication between us.
- I'm heartbroken—the situation seems hopeless.

There were also some readers who felt mothers- and fathers-in-law should do some self-reflection, too, to see where they might have overstepped their boundaries. I take that into account in this section, which is much more than a litany of grievances. Rather, it offers insights and practical solutions for easing tensions in the extended family. Read on!

What's Her Problem?

Second only to the Wicked Stepmother, the Difficult Daughter-in-Law (DDIL) looms large as a source of friction in the family. She divides mother from son, withholds grandchildren, sabotages family get-togethers, and rains misery on one and all, especially her mother-in-law (MIL). This is not to say that every MIL is perfect and every son's wife is a pain in the neck, but there are so many horror stories about the latter's shoddy behavior toward the former that I felt we needed to look into the situation.

Family of birth

According to Deborah Levinson, a licensed clinical social worker who has helped many women deal with divisive family situations, "The roots of the difficult daughter-in-law's behavior may go back to her family of birth. She might have seen her mother be disrespectful or unloving toward *her* mother-in-law. She might have been in competition with her mother for her father's attention. Now, she's transferred the power struggle to her marriage, with the husband a stand-in for her father and the mother-in-law a competitor for his love. Another explanation is that, never having developed a good sense of self-worth, she's so insecure that she feels anyone in her husband's orbit is a threat. If he has a close relationship with his mother, that could definitely play into her fears."

There may be other factors at play, too, says Levinson. "The difficult daughter-in-law may come from a family that was not affectionate, and, if her husband's family is more demonstrative, she may feel uncomfortable with their intimacy. Then, too, as she is expected to work, run a household, and be a perfect mother to her children, she may just be plain overwhelmed. Finally, we shouldn't rule out the possibility that she has a personality disorder or other psychopathology."

When her boundaries differ

Levinson and other experts contend that people have distinct ideas about boundaries and how far they should be expected to stretch theirs in order to fit in. If you've read about the Kennedy family's touch football games, you know they were exuberant. When Jackie literally wouldn't play ball, the rest of the family thought she was stuck up. Was she being a DDIL or was there just not a good fit between her literary/artistic bent and the Kennedy's rough-tumble idea of a good time?

Our society's general disrespect for older people doesn't help, either. Far from being honored for their wisdom and experience as they are in other cultures, America's "senior citizens" can be objects of ridicule. Moreover, there's the well-documented narcissism of the younger generation, who are often clueless about or unwilling to fulfill the expectations of the older generation. This is at best frustrating and at worst hurtful to parents of adult children who remember a time when all members of the extended family sat down to Sunday dinner together, phoned each other regularly, and exchanged cards and gifts on one another's special occasions—even when they weren't overly fond of one another.

That's gone. Excluding ethnic groups who have a strong sense of familial inclusion, parents are now expected to go out of their way for "the kids" rather than the other way around. Moreover, younger husbands and wives feel their only allegiance should be to their own parents rather than forming "one big happy family." In an extreme case (or maybe not), one woman I know lay gravely ill in a hospital bed for four weeks. During that whole time her daughter-in-law, who lived locally, never visited and didn't even pick up a phone—and this was not a case of hard feelings or estrangement.

How She Wreaks Havoc

In our first post on this topic, *What is Her Problem?*, we examined the many reasons *why* the difficult daughter-in-law (DDIL) makes life so miserable, especially for her mother-in-law (MIL). In this piece we'll look at I she creates tension and dissension throughout the extended family.

She can be passive-aggressive

The DDIL may appear pleasant and even meek on the surface, but her hostile actions belie this accommodating posture. She may agree to the restaurant you've picked out but spend the whole dinner pouting or playing with her food. She can be hard to make plans with and then, when she finally gives you a definite date to visit the grandchildren, she "forgets" the appointment, sometimes after you've changed your own plans to accommodate her or traveled a good distance to get there. Psychologists refer to this behavior as *passive-aggressive*, and it is frustrating and draining for those on the receiving end. It's also insidious and perversely effective: the DDIL who engages in this kind of guerrilla warfare is adept at setting up her in-laws so she doesn't have to take responsibility for her own behavior. She is always the injured party.

If she doesn't want to see her husband's family over the holidays, for example, she will not say anything directly. Rather, she will put them in the humiliating position of trying to make arrangements through their son, who will have to deliver the news that they're not going to happen. Unfortunately, speaking up against her shabby treatment doesn't seem to work very well, because it gives the DDIL

ammo to revert to her default mode, which is "put upon."
One of the DDIL's stealth moves is being unavailable.
Some parents say they practically have to serve her with
a subpoena to have her show up for a family event. Either
she has a convenient scheduling conflict or, if she does put
in an appearance, she quickly scurries off or stays on her
tablet the whole time—even during Thanksgiving dinner!
The excuse is often that she has a BIG JOB. Puhleeze . . .
even the president of General Motors doesn't work 24/7.
I've been told of DDILs who go into their bedroom after
saying hello or never even come out. I also know of a family
where the son has to bring the children to his parents' hotel
when they're visiting from out of town. But the topper is the
understanding that the in-laws can only come over when
the DDIL is off somewhere, competing in a marathon.

She can be a bully

Too often with the DDIL it's her way or the highway,
and everyone caves to keep peace in the family. She may
roll her eyes when her in-laws offer a suggestion, so they
quickly learn to nod and agree with everything she says.
Or she might lob in a zinger out of nowhere, which throws
them off balance and leads them to become even more
guarded in their speech. But the worst is when she makes
snide comments about them in front of others, even the
grandchildren, which is both humiliating and destructive.

According to Dr. Deanna Brann, author of *Reluctantly
Related: Secrets of Getting Along with your Mother-in-Law
or Daughter-in-Law*, "Unlike bullying between children
and adolescents, a DIL who bullies her MIL is really
involving the whole family. And this is where things get
complicated. As a rule the family dynamic is set up in

such a way that no one deals directly with the bullying problem. The MIL (and her side of the family) is afraid to do or say anything for fear of retribution; the DIL's husband doesn't see it, doesn't want to see it, or doesn't know what to do when he does see it; the DIL's side of the family is either in collusion knowingly or not, or they are afraid of her as well."

She uses weapons of mass destruction

The DDIL's husband will often adopt a helpless, and self-protective, stance in the midst of all the drama. Either he'll brush it off with such remarks as, "Oh, you know how she is. That's just Sandy being Sandy." Or he'll play the exasperated victim, "What do you want me to do? You handle it!" According to Dr. Brann, "If the MIL talks to her son, she puts him in the middle, and often times, he gets upset with *her* because he doesn't know what to do either, and he doesn't want to create problems at home." Parents will rationalize their son's acceptance of his wife's outrageous behavior toward them by saying: "Oh, well, he's happy; that's all that counts."

The worst, of course, is when the DDIL plays games with the grandparent/grandchild relationship. Whether it's insisting that her mother-in-law can only visit if she or her husband is around—and only if they're not busy with other, more important matters—or imposing strict (and even off-the-wall) guidelines, what should be a cozy visit can feel like a recon mission through a mine field. Although Grandma might not have fed her son strictly organic, let him watch TV, and made him put his napkin on his lap, somehow he grew up and the DDIL married him. But that's neither here nor there to someone bent on asserting her power.

Where's Her Husband?

The Difficult Daughter-in-Law (DDIL) is the bane of many parents of grown offspring. From the comments on our website and the huge number of clicks this topic gets on the Internet, it's obviously an open sore that may scab over but never heals. I looked at the DDIL's behavior in three earlier articles, and now I'm turning my attention to her husband-your-son. According to the literature, parents who have written in, and experts in the field, generally speaking if your son is married to a DDIL, he's at best missing in action and at worst breaking your heart.

A mother's heartbreak

This comment posted to the POGO website is representative:

"It's such a painful situation to be in. My DIL has managed to paint me as a monster and has the ability to get my son to ignore everything I have done for him and her as well as forgiving all the hurt she has caused, all the trouble she has stirred in the family and all the bile she has vomited over us all. I put up with her for his sake, but she tells him such lies about me and plays the victim and he believes her.

She comes from a confrontational and argumentative background. She sees weakness in compromise and forgiveness and strength in aggression and manipulation. The really sad thing about all this is that my son cannot see her for the divisive, duplicitous person she is. I have cried buckets over this. I hope I am now coming to terms with the reality that the son I raised is no longer a part of my life, and I have zero control over that. My love for him has and will never change, but the dynamic that once existed between us is no longer there, and sometimes I even hear her words and her arrogance come from my son's mouth. It's like I don't really know him anymore."

According to Deborah Levinson, a licensed clinical social worker who frequently deals with these situations in her private practice, "The DDIL married your son because she could control him, and if she has the power in the family, she rules the roost. It's too dangerous to try to realign the husband/wife relationship. Besides which, if you get into a power struggle with your son's toxic wife, you will lose."

Analyze the situation

Ms. Levinson suggests taking a step back and asking yourself these questions:

1. Who has the power in the family?

2. How is your son doing outside the marriage? If his self-esteem is low, he may be more prone to acquiesce to his wife's antics.

3. Where are the boundaries between generations and between husband and wife?

4. What are the rules of the family?

5. Where are the triangles? Are you being used as a wedge to defuse tension between your son and his wife?

6. Are there ways your son can get some of your needs met without rocking the boat in his marriage?

"You are playing a sophisticated game of chess here," Ms. Levinson says. "You need to try to find ways to have a relationship with your son that doesn't threaten his wife.

She advises:

- Take a fresh look at the situation.
- Check your ego at the door. One grandfather even agreed to supervised visits with his grandsons because that was the only way he could get access to them.
- Keep your eyes on the prize—access and normality.
- Let go of any expectations.
- If your son has children, ask him to make sure they know you have value. Keep communicating with the kids in any way you can, because each contact is an imprint.
- Look for small ways to make inroads. Ask your son for input as to how you can give his wife what she needs so she will open the door just a smidgeon.

The worst scenario, of course, is when the DDIL weaponizes her children, either keeping her husband's parents away and/or turning the kids against them. This was the case with one of our readers who was barred from seeing her grandchildren for a decade. She posted: "At the end (of their marriage) my daughter-in-law tried to forbid us from attending the children's college graduations, and SHE PUT THAT INTO THE DIVORCE AGREEMENT! Thank God, our son refused, he's now marrying a lovely, wonderful, sweet woman, and we're back in touch with our grandchildren. To all of you I say: Hang in there!"

Too Much Information

Meg's daughter-in-law, Dana, keeps complaining to her about Nicky, her husband of two years. Dana says Nicky is a slob, a spendthrift, and a poor provider. Meg doesn't want to hear these stories, which cast her son in a poor light and might signal the end of the kids' marriage. Nicky knows that Dana badmouths him to Meg, and it's driving a wedge between mother and son. What should Meg do?

- *Listen sympathetically but keep mum?*
- *Tell Dana to put a cork in it?*
- *Point out the consequences of his behavior to Nicky?*

The Panel Weighs In:

Cristina: *These young marrieds need couples counseling. Dana complaining to Meg might help her let off steam, but it's not helping their marriage. I'm not averse to Meg's speaking to Nicky, either.*

Bob: *Dana needs to speak directly to Nicky. Meg could be helpful in encouraging them to seek counseling together in a safe environment.*

Ethan: *Boundaries, boundaries, boundaries! Meg needs to let her daughter-in-law know that it's not okay to talk down her son, which his having a harmful effect on others in the family as well as her own marriage.*

Louella: *Dana is looking for support and an ally. It's never a good idea to choose sides, though, as it could boomerang against Meg.*

It's a Family Affair

The mother-in-law (MIL)—daughter-in-law (DIL) relationship is key to extended family harmony, and when it goes awry everyone is negatively affected. As Deanna Brann, Ph.D. pointed out in her book, *Reluctantly Related Revisited*, "The DIL may be thinking *His mother won't let go*; while the MIL might be thinking, *The MIL wants to keep him from his family*." Dr. Brann feels that competition between the two women, possibly unacknowledged or mislabeled is behind the tension. Nevertheless, in one way or another everyone in the extended family is affected—and scarred—by the feud between the two women.

Men avoid conflict

For the men in the family, there is only frustration, as we saw in *Where's Her Husband?* Caught in the middle between his mother and his wife, the DIL's husband (the MIL's son) feels like the rope in a tug of war. His loyalties are divided, and he knows he'll be the loser no matter who "wins." His brother might be upset with him if the DIL has tried to enlist his wife (her sister-in-law) in the battle, which she might or might not want to join. While the brother wants to shield his wife from the conflict, he wants even more for the situation to just go away, and he resents his sister-in-law for stirring the pot. Similarly, the MIL's husband is upset for his wife and angry with his daughter-in-law. "Oh, why can't we all just get along?" is the men's prevailing sentiment.

The other women in the family will probably be called upon to choose up sides, too. Looking for reinforcement, the DIL may enlist her sister-in-law as a confidante and ally against a common enemy. The MIL's daughter will be similarly drafted for the other side to assure her mother that she's blameless and it's all the DIL's fault for causing disharmony in the family. This may pit the younger woman against both her brother and sister-in-law if it becomes all-out war.

DIL's family weighs in

Then, too, there's the DIL's family of origin, who just hear her version of the story. Since, as it is said, "blood is thicker than water," they also line up behind her. Based on what they've been told and what experiences and emotions they bring to bear, they may make suggestions or embark upon actions that only add fuel to the fire.

Finally, there are the grandchildren who may not understand the issues, but who can definitely feel the tension between two people whom they love. It's upsetting for them because they have a deep, primal relationship with their mother and, often, with their grandmother.

The main actors in these scenarios are not usually aware of the hurt they are inflicting on others in the family, so consumed are they with feeling put-upon and in the right. Still, the experts say, what counts is not who is at fault, but who is willing to reach out first to improve the situation."

His Wife Won't Work

The Romos' son, Tony, lost his business and went bankrupt a year ago. The Romos know Tony has been struggling ever since to pay the bills, but his wife, Sandra, a trained dental hygienist, refuses to work, even part-time. Tony and Sandra only have one child at home now, an independent high school junior, but Sandra still refuses to pitch in. Her position is that they had an agreement that Tony would be the breadwinner and she would be the stay-at-home mom. If Tony can't provide, she's feels it's up to her in-laws to keep them afloat—and in the style to which she is accustomed. The Romos don't want to add marital discord to their son's woes, but this situation is killing them emotionally and financially. What should the Romos do?

- Urge Tony to stand up to Sandra?
- Slip hints to her that it would set a great example for the kids to see them all pull together as a family in this crisis?
- Stay out of it?

The Panel Weighs In:

Leslie: It is not the Romos' obligation to shore up this adult family when the wife is perfectly capable of helping out financially. I can see why they're beside themselves!

Henry: The Romos can only hope that when Sandra sees her lifestyle crumble, she'll get off her rear. If the Romos subsidize her and Tony, they're just prolonging a dysfunctional situation.

D'mai: *The Romos might provide short-term assistance, but they have to steadily reduce the amount and/or set a firm deadline for the "gifts" or "loans" to stop altogether. They'll feel better about the situation if there's an end in sight.*

Phil: *The Romos' gift to their son should be a counseling session with a financial adviser—with Sandra and possibly even the high school junior in tow. It's time for all of them to grow up and face the reality of the bankruptcy as a family.*

What Mothers-in-Law Wish They Could Tell Their Daughters-in-Law

by Donne Davis

L et's face it: communication with adult children can be challenging. But, communication with adult children-in-law can be even more challenging, especially daughters-in-law. Many grandmas may relate to the mother-in-law in this story:

A brand new grandma is standing in her daughter-in-law's kitchen protectively cradling her tiny granddaughter. She's in pure rhapsody as she drinks in the yummy smells of the newborn baby girl, imagining her saying: "Grandmom, I know you and love you already."

Then her daughter-in-law shatters the euphoric mood by screeching: "Don't hold her like that!" and grabs the infant from grandmom's arms, placing her in her infant seat.

It doesn't matter that this new grandmother raised four children of her own, or that she would sacrifice every part of her being for this new child, or that she purchased the seat that now substituted for her embrace. This woman knew there was nothing she could say because once you become a grandmother, you will find yourself virtually speechless. To alienate your daughter-in-law might result in losing access to your grandchild. (This scenario is from Ellie Slott Fisher's book, *It's Either Her or Me: A Guide to Help a Mom and Her Daughter-in-Law Get Along.*)

The mother and daughter-in-law relationship can be fragile or tense when the grown man in the middle must show his loyalty to his wife and put his mother second. If the mother-in-law can accept that her son's wife is now the primary relationship, then she will succeed in building a mutually respectful relationship.

What mothers-in-law want

Writer Mary May Larmoyeux of *Family Life* asked her friends, "What do you wish you could tell your daughter-in-law?" Here are the themes that emerged from their responses:

- **Although my relationship with my son has changed, remember that I am still his mother.** Be considerate of the fact that I used to be the woman in his life.

- **Accept me for who I am.** Realize that I may do things differently and try to understand my ways.

- **Please respect my age and experience.** I would like to be able to share some of my experience with you without offending you.

- **Talk with me about hard things.** If you are feeling hurt by something I did or said, find a way to gently bring it up.

- **Try to understand**. Don't judge. There are two sides to any story.

- **Remember, we are family.** Please include me in some of your family activities and traditions.

- **Communicate with me.** I'd love to tell you more about my son's childhood—please ask me.

- **Get to know me as a person.** Find things that we have in common and let's enjoy them together.
- **Express expectations clearly.** It would help if you told me the best ways that I could help you.
- **Help me know my grandchildren.** I want to be a part of my grandchild's life and love it when you regularly share pictures.
- **Take time to express gratitude.** Taking the time to express your appreciation for what I do means a lot to me.
- **Thank you!** You understand my son better than I do and I thank God for you.

Some mothers-and daughters-in-law form close friendships very quickly. They realize they share a common bond in loving the same man. For others, this may take years. But most do want to connect with each other. They want to find common ground. They want to know each other as individual women with feelings, beliefs, and ideas. After all, it's not a contest.

Mothers-in-law should be available, but not interfering and respectful of their daughters-in-law. And the daughter-in-law should realize that in this vast world, few people will ever come close to loving and caring for her child the way she does—one of those people is her mother-in-law.

Donne Davis is the founder of GaGa Sisterhood and author of When Being a Grandma Isn't So Grand: 4 Keys to L.O.V.E. Your Grandchild's Parents.

How *Not* to Sweat the Small Stuff with Your Daughter-in-Law

by Deanna Brann, PhD

How many times has your daughter-in-law done something or said something that just makes your blood boil and you can't seem to let it go? You keep replaying it over and over in your head, and the more you think about it the angrier or more hurt you feel. In fact, you find you can't *stop* thinking about it. We all have experienced this at one time or another. Even if you don't say anything to your daughter-in-law at the time, her actions affect your relationship because the bad feelings you *think* you are covering up end up coming out through your behavior. Trust me, even if you are sure this isn't true, it probably is. As much as you want to believe you can hide those bad feelings, you really can't.

Relutant to make waves

Let me give you an example. Let's say your daughter-in-law says something to you that really hurts your feelings. You don't want to say anything because you don't want to make waves and you don't think it is worth the time to talk about it. You think to yourself, *Wow, that hurt, but I'm just going to let it go,* even though you're really hurt by what was said. So what do you do? The typical reaction is to withdraw emotionally. You get quiet, a bit reserved. Pulling back feels natural because if you don't, you're afraid you might say something, which is what you're trying to avoid—not to mention the fact that you feel the need to protect yourself from being hurt again. Your daughter-in-law, sensing a change in your actions and feeling tension that didn't exist before, may ask you if something is wrong, or she may say nothing at all. Either way you choose to stay quiet as an attempt to "let it go." But now your jaw is tight, you don't make eye contact, and your tone of voice is abrupt. Regardless of what you actually *say*, she can feel that something is up because of the *way* you say it (including not just your tone but also your body language). And of course, this then affects the relationship.

Keeping in negative feelings

Hanging onto those feelings and stewing about them also affects *you*. After all, you're the one who keeps the anger, frustration, and hurt (or whatever you're feeling) alive, churning away. Whether or not she meant to be hurtful you're the one who gets stuck in these negative feelings—not your daughter-in-law.

You may think I'm going to encourage you to speak your peace, but realistically speaking, that isn't always the answer. Sometimes that can make the situation worse. So when you decide saying something isn't going to help, how can you stop sweating the small stuff for the sake of the relationship? Here are some tips that will help:

1. **Take an emotional step backward.** Create some distance for yourself so you can look at the situation more objectively.

2. **Don't assume what your daughter-in-law said or did was a personal attack against you.** It is very

possible that it has nothing to do with you at all—maybe you just happened to be in the line of fire at the time.

3. **Look at the feelings you are having and ask yourself how they are serving you.** For example, does the fact that you feel hurt or angry help you justify how you feel towards your daughter-in-law? Does it allow you to feel *better* about yourself, feel that you are right (and so she is wrong), or feel justified in some other way? If so, how does this help the relationship?

If these feelings, instead, leave you feeling *bad* about yourself, is that particular feeling familiar in some way—have you felt this way with *other* people who have mattered to you? If so, then your daughter-in-law's actions may have less to do with how you feel than you think (after all you've experienced this very same feeling with other important people in your life).

4. **What is *one* thing you can do for yourself that can shift your painful feelings?** You only have to do one thing to get your feelings to *start* shifting in a new direction—just one thing! You don't have to have all the answers, just figure out *one* thing to do differently to start this shift. Take that first *small* step and then you'll feel better able to take another small step. And on it goes until you've moved passed the bad feelings. But, remember, you have to start somewhere and that's with one small step.

So the next time you are in an awkward or unpleasant situation with your daughter-in-law, don't stew about it. If you decide it's best to deal with the situation yourself by moving beyond your feelings, use these four tips and stop sweating the small stuff!

And beyond this…

One of the key things you can do to make your relationship with your daughter-in-law better and less likely to get into these tense situations is to develop a relationship with her that is independent of your son and grandchildren. As you get to know her and she gets to know you a personal connection develops. You are not just—"My husband's mother," but instead a person who matters.

Deanna Brann, PhD, is the author of Your In-Law Survival Guide, Reluctantly Related, *and* Reluctantly Related Revisited. *She can be reached at www.drdeannabrann.com.*

How to Communicate with Distant and Uncommunicative In-Laws

by Pamela Reynolds

There are many reasons why a mother- and a daughter-in-law are quiet or reserved around each other. At times, people overstep the boundaries others have set up for them. That causes one party to be angry with the other. The resentment occurs when we believe someone has unrightfully entered our space and we want justice. Sometimes that can mean atonement. None of us thinks about the times when we tread on others, but if it happens to us it becomes a different and powerful story. It can lead one down the path of unreasonable behavior and sometimes revenge.

When mothers-in-law say too much

Have you ever gone to a party and spoken your mind? Did you later regret some of what you said? The words that mothers-in-law use are sometimes loaded with an instructive, controlling tone. They don't mean to sound this way, but mothers have been teaching their offspring for so many years that it is difficult to stop all the advice at once. Yet, stopping is what must be done if one is to keep peace and allow their son to be liberated. Daughters-in-law resent most—or all—unwanted advice and don't want to be told they are wrong. In all actuality, nobody likes to be told they are wrong.

As hard as it is, the mother-in-law must learn to let her adult children make their own way, even if to her it is plain clear that they are making mistakes. Nothing will irritate a daughter-in-law more than interfering with her and her husband's business.

Mothers-in-law can say too little

There is the other extreme for mothers-in-law—to say too little. This happens when a mother-in-law is hurt with all the insults that result from her mild, or not so mild, interference. As a result, she is wounded and reacts by staying outside of the normal conversation people are having. This only upsets her son and his wife even more. They take her behavior as a strategy to place them on the defensive.

We may not notice that we are building borders around ourselves and hiding behind a tall wall of good intentions. In the meantime, our son and his wife are constructing their own fences and keeping us out. Is that what we really want? Saying too much does cause issues, but saying too little makes people assume you are thinking the worst. After all, neither of these scenarios counts as cooperating with your in-law.

Being a martyr doesn't work

As an extreme strategy, many mothers- and daughters-in-law become the martyr and assume they will gain attention. There is no positive outcome to be found, however. Everyone sees through the acting, and they resent the attempt to garner support in such a manner. The bond in an in-law relationship is found at a place in the middle, where both parties need to meet. Unfortunately, that is the hardest area for us to visit because it's important for us to think that everything we say and do is always correct.

As we grow into adulthood, we discover that throughout any given day we are wrong and right many times. Who cares how many times we were wrong? That is the question we should ask.

Atonement can equate to punishment

The trouble appears when a mother- or daughter-in-law is punished for speaking too much or too little. Once we have offended an in-law, we must pick up the pieces of the relationship and try to put it back together. If we refuse to forgive or apologize, we only add to the pain that has already been experienced. I have often heard people say, "I know I am not always right but..." If we truly believe that is true, then we can all agree that we do make mistakes and require forgiveness.

Likewise, there are times when each of us has been correct, and that leaves us with the job of offering forgiveness to someone else. If we want forgiveness, we ought to be willing to offer it to others. Making a mother-in-law or daughter-in-law pay over and over for something she did can add to our own baggage and leave us exhausted in the end. It is far better to dump the anger, anxiety and bad feelings. Nobody wants to carry that baggage around.

Mistakes grant us the opportunity to learn

We learn the most when making mistakes. The next step is to choose to walk a different road when again confronted with the same problem. The desire to say or do something when you are not asked to contribute is a lesson better learned early. It gets easier every time you are successful at maintaining neutrality.

You don't have to be angry with yourself. After so many years of teaching—because you are a parent—it is not easy to let go of your instinct to give advice. It is still relevant that you keep trying until you succeed.

Courage and compromise allow us to make peace

It takes honesty and courage to see and accept our errors. It takes compromise from both sides to make amends and bring about peace. When countries make peace, they gain and lose, but the powerful result is worthwhile to all because they have gained harmony. Likewise, none of us can make our mother- or daughter-in-law disappear, nor would we want our son or husband to suffer the pain if we could.

What we can do is gather our courage and work on a solution that leads to peace for everyone. If we expect our world, country, city or community to find peace, then we must begin within our homes and, especially, within ourselves.

Pamela Reynolds writes about relationships on her website, www.pamreynolds.me. She is the author of The Princess and the Queen, Simpikins, *and* J is for Jail.

When You Don't Feel Welcome

L*ily and Barry's son, Peter, is married to Jill, a woman who insults them and does not make them feel welcome in her home. From what they can see, Peter—with whom they have a very loving relationship—never chides Jill for her behavior toward his parents. Since Lily and Barry don't want to alienate their only son, they take what she dishes out, but it hurts them to the core.*

- *Should they confront Peter?*
- *Tell off Jill?*
- *Pretend everything is honky dory to keep the peace?*

The Panel Weighs In:

Cyndi: *I'm a pacifist—and an optimist. If they can keep playing along, Jill may stop feeling so threatened by her in-laws and start behaving like a decent person.*

Chris: *No, the leopard does not change its spots. To maintain their own self-respect, Lily and Barry have to tell Jill that her insults are not okay.*

T.J.: *Lily and Barry should definitely NOT confront their son. That would make him choose a side and they would lose.*

Alan: *Perhaps the parents could have a regular date with their son out of his house, because half a relationship is better than none at all.*

5 Ways to Deal with Uneasy Mother/Daughter-in-Law Moments

by Pamela Reynolds

We all find it so easy to blame others when a relationship fails. If we could read our daughter-in-law's mind, we would likely find she is blaming us for the uneasy atmosphere. The truth is, both parties sabotage the relationship when they assume, judge and expect certain things to happen. Getting off to a bad start makes everyone uneasy.

The tension is strong, and both women are lost in their own thoughts. Before the night is over, they speak cordially but make brief contact with each other. It is easy to get caught up in the drama which serves nobody and adds to the confusion. Here are 5 ways to deal with the mother- and daughter-in-law "elephant in the room."

At times, both women can simply be misguided in their thoughts and judgements of a situation. That is the best kept secret. Neither woman wants to upset the elephant in the room, so neither discusses any real issues or problems they have. Mothers- and daughters-in-law have individual fears, as well as desires. Daughters-in-law want to control their lives and their children. Mothers-in-law feel the same way, but their son is grown up. Control becomes impossible, so the mother-in-law must see the changed playing field.

The mother-in-law fears losing her relationship with her son and grandchildren. She sometimes pushes for what she perceives as her rights, and she makes matters worse. The daughter-in-law feels threatened and fights back with refusals to visit. Both women dig in their heels and ignore the man-in-the-middle's suffering. Be open, honest and communicate with your daughter-in-law without assuming or judging. Don't expect to gain all you want, but instead, appreciate what you get and more will flow to you.

Don't count the time you share with your grandchildren but do count the love!

Nobody wants to make children unhappy, and kids want and deserve love from everyone. As much as we give and love our children, adding more love to their lives through other people is important. We should understand that grandchildren lose the most when grandparents are not allowed to engage with them. When they are grown they may question our reasons for keeping grandma and papa at a distance from them.

Children ask many questions when they are young, but they ask more questions when they are older. They will not be deceived. Kids deserve all the love and attention they can get. Refuse to put them in the middle of your arguments because they thrive on love and attention.

Let parents set the boundaries

Parents should set boundaries and rules as well as times people can visit. Grandparents must be flexible about the restrictions and accept what they receive. With three daughters-in-law and one son-in-law, I have found that the more I accept the conditions the parents set, the more lenient the parents become. That is a fact. The grandchildren tell me about their visits with their other grandmas and papas, and I cherish the conversation. I am sure they do the same about their visits with me. Children are open and carefree, and they hold nothing back. The parents and grandparents have peace and are surrounded by the loving atmosphere. This is the result of open communication, which we all strive to achieve, and the ability to share without jealousy. It turns gossip into discussions, judgements into tolerance and assumptions into trust. It is never perfect and has its flaws, but it is positive, honest and worth the effort.

Always offer praise in some form

Gossip hurts, demeans and causes unending hardships. Most of gossip is hearsay or half-truths. Even gossip that is true serves only to bring pain and misunderstanding. If you want people to speak kindly of you, you should speak gently of others.

You won't have to eat your words or be embarrassed when someone repeats your indiscretion. Recall the adage that what we see in others may be rampant in us. I have often learned this lesson by committing the same mistake I criticized another for. It is unnerving to find the fault within one's self—but very enlightening.

Work on creating a harmonious relationship

In any harmonious relationship the interactions are easy, unguarded and contain more humor. The conversation is relaxed, the stress and anxiety are not present, and the subjects of conversation are varied and interesting. When the visit is over we are filled with a sense of joy. Maintaining a good relationship is for the benefit of all.

We can focus on what is good about each other, and

learn to tolerate what we don't like. Mothers-in-law can help with babysitting, cleaning the dishes after enjoying a meal or shopping with their daughter-in-law to again help with the children. Offering to drive or pick something up is also helpful. The daughter-in-law may offer to help with dishes, visit or spend a day or evening in an outing with the mother-in-law. Even if it is tense in the beginning of a relationship, put the effort into creating magic and forming a devoted bond. It is so beneficial for both women and therapeutic in so many ways.

The changes are never what we imagine

Don't measure or imagine. There is only one you and nobody else like you. Your experiences, ideas, jobs and talents are unique, and your grandchildren benefit from this.

If you can admit that you love all your children the same, then you can trust that your grandchildren love all their grandparents. If you compare and measure then you will always distrust and feel loss. If you unconditionally love and are grateful for the love you have in your life, then you will never be disappointed.

Pamela Reynolds writes about relationships on her website, www.pamreynolds.me. She is the author of The Princess and the Queen, Simpikins, *and* J is for Jail.

Picking Up the Tab

Their son's in-laws, the McGoverns, are "generous to a fault." Trudy and Jeff never knew what that expression meant until they found themselves at the receiving end of many expensive family dinners—for which the McGoverns insisted on paying. Trudy and Jeff aren't poor, but they are beginning to feel like the poor relations. How should they handle it?

- *Should Trudy and Jeff try to put a stop to the McGoverns' largesse?*
- *Decline their invitations?*
- *Insist on paying half?*

The Panel Weighs In:

Maureen: *Trudy and Jeff should get to pick the restaurant from time to time, saying "It's our turn now." Treating at fancy restaurants may be a power play on the McGoverns' part, and Trudy and Jeff need to call a halt to it if it bothers them.*

Leon: *They should insist on paying half and give the kids a not-so-subtle hint that they should occasionally chip in, too.*

Frank: *If it makes the McGoverns feel good treating the family, let them. They can obviously afford it, so Trudy and Jeff should sit back and enjoy their generosity.*

Susan: *Trudy and Jeff should hand the maître d' their credit card as they come in and tell him they're picking up the check that night.*

Reader's Comment

Call me paranoid. The generosity of buying expensive anything puts the recipients in a difficult position. My own parents were so very generous that at times I felt guilty because I was never in a position to reciprocate. Of course, it was neither expected nor requested. However, later in life, I was able to give back in nonmonetary ways. Trips to doctor visits, brief visits to check on them, made sure grandson knew them, invited them for at-home celebrations, notes of thanks and love. S.C.

How to Make It Better

As difficult as your daughter-in-law may be, don't give up hope! If you wallow and succumb to negativity, it's going to be that much harder to improve the situation. The experts agree that change will probably have to start with you. Here's what they advise:

- **Figure out why things started to go south.** There's power in just acknowledging to the DDIL that you understand why she might have interpreted a situation the way she did. She's as afraid of losing her position in the family as you are.

- **Step back and take a deep breath.** If the DDIL feels threatened by you, less might be more for a while. You could stay in touch at arm's length via text or just have a time-out altogether. It might be more productive to wait until things simmer down before you start to try mending fences.

- **Choose your confidants carefully.** When you're sick at heart, it's natural to want to unburden yourself. But be careful whom you choose to take into your confidence. If you talk down your DIL to other family members, they may feel they have to choose between the two of you or start to think of you as a bitter, old woman. The last thing you want to do is insist they choose sides. What if they choose her?

- **Look for solutions as well as validation.**
  Sometimes everyone needs to vent, but it's so much
  more productive to look for ways to unfreeze a
  situation rather than just repeating all the outrages
  and injustices you've suffered at the DDIL's hand.

- **Try a new twist on some old ideas.** When you're
  stuck and your confidants make suggestions, don't
  reject them out of hand. Look at the overtures you
  might make with fresh eyes. Yes, you've tried them
  and they failed before, but that was then and this is
  now. Where there's life there's hope.

- **Negativity is your enemy, positivity your friend.**
  It's easy to say, "Been there, done that," but
  clinging to an entrenched position blocks thinking
  creatively about how to make things better.
  Moreover, what are you getting out of holding to
  your fixed position? It's salve to your wounds to
  wallow in victimhood, but it won't get you where
  you want to be—a family member with a good
  relationship with ALL the other family members. It
  isn't easy, but it is sure worth the fight.

Apologies: How to Make Them Work

When things go sour between the generations, mothers- and fathers-in-law may not even realize what, if anything, they've done wrong. They truly don't know how they could have so offended their daughter-in-law that she won't even talk to them anymore. What they do know is that they want to get the unpleasantness behind them and restore harmony to the family as quickly as possible. The question is how to do it? The experts say the key is apologizing, but only if it's done in the right way and in the spirit of forgiveness and reconciliation. Here's what they recommend:

- **Be Sincere.** You have to express genuine regret and be remorseful that you caused your daughter-in-law to be unhappy. Only genuine emotion will restore your relationship, they say. The pros point out that true sincerity is a proven way to resolve disputes and dissipate negative emotions quickly and effectively.

- **Be Prompt.** If a specific incident triggered the acrimony, try to set things right as quickly as possible. Too little, too late may doom your efforts from the start. The experts say that giving an apology as early as possible leads to less conflict later on and increases satisfaction on both sides of a dispute.

- **Let your daughter-in-law know she's being heard.** Mediators say that often disputants care more about airing their grievances than winning. That's why in your apology it's a good idea to show that you take

her issues seriously, even if privately you think they're
without merit.

- **Keep it specific.** If an apology is totally generic,
  chances are it won't be effective. Allude to the points
  of contention between the two of you and offer to
  do your part in setting them right. Also, be concrete
  about your planned corrective actions.

- **Focus on the harm you might have caused.**
  Minimize the context, motivation, or justification for
  your actions while keeping the spotlight squarely on
  the act itself. "I'm sorry I said that; it was insensitive
  of me" is called for. "I'm sorry you were offended
  by . . ." is not. In fact, it's a non-apology. According
  to Harriet Lerner, Ph.D., author of *Why Won't You
  Apologize?: Healing Big Betrayals and Everyday Hurts*:
  "You should own your behavior and *apologize* for
  it, period." She warns against sounding defensive or
  overemphasizing your own pain or remorse, which
  minimizes the other person's hurt.

- **Don't use the word "but."** According to Dr. Lerner,
  "'But' automatically cancels out an apology, and nearly
  always introduces a criticism or excuse." This isn't the
  time to pass judgment but to acknowledge how your
  actions might have offended our daughter-in-law and
  that you're sorry for them.

- **See things from her perspective.** You may feel that
  you're being accused of crimes you never committed
  or that your daughter-in-law is blowing little
  annoyances into major offenses. This is maddening,
  but if you want to unfreeze the situation, the experts
  urge you to step into your daughter-in-law's shoes.
  Trying to understand where she's coming from will

help you move the ball forward in a way nothing else could.

- **Never mind who "started it."** To make your apology effective, it should refrain from assigning blame. Even if you're only slightly or not at all to blame and/or were justifiably provoked, you can still say simply, "I'm sorry for my part in this." Too often each side wants to convince the other of his/her righteous position, which is a losing proposition. Of course, serious hurt requires time and work to overcome, but a sincere "I'm sorry" is an excellent place to begin.

Chapter 2

Grandparenting–or Not

Some of the issues that arise for today's grandparents are difficult, whether caused by the difficult daughter-in-law or not. Thankfully, most are joyous. That's why, although National Grandparents Day is always celebrated on the Sunday after Labor Day, every day is Grandparents Day at POGO.

As I was growing up, my paternal grandparents were a big part of my life. I lived across the street from them until I was seven years old and spent a lot of time at their house even after we moved away. The benefits of this experience were incalculable and lasted a lifetime. My grandparents were from the old country, which gave me the opportunity to see people drinking tea through a sugar cube clamped between front teeth, hear songs of the Russian army, learn knitting and sewing, and observe how a fig tree is kept alive through a harsh New York winter.

Professionally, being close to my grandparents resulted in my first book, *America Fever: The Story of American Immigration*. Personally, it always made me comfortable with older people and accepting of the fact that I would become an older person, too. Above all, my grandparents' unconditional love made me feel valued, embedded, secure. When I became a grandparent myself, I felt the joy of giving the same "love without baggage" to my children's children or, as my grandfather-the-businessman called them, "interest on interest."

59

Grandparenting: A Win-Win for All

"Truth be told, being a grandma is as close as we ever get to perfection. The ultimate warm sticky bun with plump raisins and nuts. Clouds nine, ten, and eleven."

Bryna Nelson Paston

Today's 65 million grandparents are not what grandparents used to be, and that's all to the good. We're living longer, healthier lives, so we can expect to be grandparents for a long time and perhaps even great-grandparents. Increasingly, we have second careers, we are traveling for business and fun, and we are actively engaged in sports and civic and philanthropic endeavors. Our independence means we can be companions to our grandchildren instead of, as in the old days, being a burden to them. It also means we're not always as available.

"When I'm ready to go home after a visit with my grandsons, the six-year-old says, "I wish you could stay for 100 days." His dad, my son, looks on, panic-stricken at the thought of even one more day with us hanging around."

Mark Sherman

But then our grown children aren't the same, either. They need more help as nuclear families are under increasing stress. We often provide the unpaid babysitting that allows single parents or two-earner households to cope. We chip in financially, and not just for frills. In divorce situations, it is often the grandparents who hold the family together.

*"Becoming a grandmother is wonderful. One
moment you're just a mother. The next you are
all-wise and prehistoric."*
Pam Brown

As you can see from the quotes I've included, for many grandparents, this role is the highlight of their lives, especially when their grandchildren are very young. Grandparenting gives us a chance to do it all over again but this time with a free heart and clear mind. We can have all the fun of parenting that we might have missed out on when we were frazzled young marrieds with young kids and demanding jobs. Grandparenting expands our circle of loved ones and provides an opportunity to grow closer to our grown children as we bond over this miracle of new life. Conversely, grandparents who are unable to maintain contact with their grandchildren due to divorce or disagreements are likely to suffer from physical illness, depression, and even grief.

*"Young people need something stable to hang on
to — a culture connection, a sense of their own
past, a hope for their own future. Most of all,
they need what grandparents can give them."*
Jay Kesler

As wonderful it is for us to have grandchildren, which some have called "God's compensation for aging," it's equally wonderful for them. They gain a sense of security and personal history because, when you think about it, grandparents stand at the nexus of five generations. We are the cultural link to the past, and we help kids feel rooted. Since we are living, breathing models of healthy aging, hopefully with them we can change the stereotype of the "elderly." Moreover, as we age before their eyes, we are giving them an opportunity to develop empathy. Finally, who doesn't need what grandparents provide in abundance: unconditional love, kindness, patience, comfort, and life lessons?

> *"To have three delightful people so genuinely*
> *and completely happy to see me is something*
> *I haven't felt since their dads were little boys.*
> *I never tired of hearing 'Daddy!' And hearing*
> *'Grandpa' never gets old, even as I do."*
>
> Mark Sherman

So, the bottom line is that they need us and we need them. In her psychology of aging classes, Susan Krauss Whitbourne, Ph.D. noted that students in her class often spoke of how important their grandparents were in their lives and how, when a student reported a death, it was generally with great sadness. According to Dr. Whitbourne, "Students value their relationships with their grandparents more than anyone realizes."

> *"You are the sun, Grandma, you are the sun in*
> *my life."*
>
> Kitty Tsui

As the Legacy Project concludes: "At their best, relationships across generations are defined in the often-used symbol of holding hands. A grandmother may hold her little granddaughter's hand as they cross the street. Thirty years later, it is the adult granddaughter taking her frail grandmother's hand. But they are still holding hands. It is a relationship that has withstood the tests of age and time."

On Call

Myrna and James McCauley have what can best be called a "transactional" relationship with their daughter-in-law, Gina. Gina is barely civil to them unless she wants something, and right now what she wants is for them to babysit her two young teenage boys—and cart them to all their activities—while she and their son take a trip abroad. Although Myrna and James dearly love their grandsons, they do not want to suspend their own activities, fly 1,000 miles from home, and spend two weeks in Tulsa, where they know nobody. They deeply resent the expectation that they will, of course, drop everything when Gina snaps her fingers although she's perennial ungracious to them. What should the McCauley's do:

- *Respectfully decline and risk alienating their son?*
- *Say yes but let Gina know they don't appreciate her attitude?*
- *Just fly out and zip their lips?*

The Panel Weighs In:

Sue: *They know they're going to do what they always do: Say yes, grouse to one another, and then paste on big smiles while they arrive in Tulsa.*

James: *There's no sense talking to Gina; her attitude is never going to change. The McCauleys just have to wait it out until the boys grow up and they can have a direct relationship with them instead of going through their mother.*

Paul: *They should kick Gina to the curb.*

Cindy: *The McCauleys certainly shouldn't bring up Gina's crummy attitude with their son, who will defend his wife to the death, as he should. Luckily, they have each other.*

Readers' Comments

They can tell their daughter-in-law (and son) that they would love to have the grandkids—in their own home, at dates which are suitable for them too. In other words, if the son and daughter-in-law want to go away without the kids, they have to communicate and mutually agree on a time and place which is also good for the grandparents. J.G.

These grandparents must find the strength to confront Gina and let her know it's not ok to assume they'll babysit for her. They love the kids but they have their own lives. Gina is selfish and will resist but so be it. S.B.

Can the parents say "NO"? Have they ever even tried? Their son and daughter-in-law should be made to realize they are too old to accommodate these demands. C.R.

I believe grandparents have as much right to a quality life as their children or grandchildren. Therefore, there should be no problem in their declining and simply speaking their truth—of course in a loving way. A.P.

Bringing Home Baby

*"One of the most powerful handclasps is that
of a new grandbaby around the finger of a
grandfather."*
—Joy Hargrove

The arrival of a grandchild, especially the first one, is a combination of taking gold at the Olympics, winning an Academy Award, and receiving the Nobel Peace Prize. In short, grandparents are over the moon. But, as we've so often noted on these pages, where there are people, there are problems or at least issues to be negotiated. Here is what we learned from the experts and new grandparents about how to make things go smoothly.

- **Be frank.** Tell the parents-to-be to what extent you'd like to be involved and how much you can handle physically. Ask them to be honest with you, too, about whether they want you in the delivery room—or even at the hospital—for the birth, when they want you to visit, and if they want you to stay over. Don't be surprised (and try not to be offended) if they opt for time alone to bond as a family, sometimes referred to as a "babymoon," or if your daughter-in-law wants her own mother there and not you.

- **Be mindful.** Even if you do get the go-ahead to visit right away, the experts advise you to stay at a nearby motel instead of in their home, if possible. Thanks to a combination of sleep deprivation and the responsibilities of a new baby, nerves can be frayed in the beginning. If you do stay over, let your offspring set the duration of your visit. Chrissy C. initially spent 12 days getting her daughter and son-in-law settled in with their twins. "Since then I only come for long weekends, and I calendar these visits according to what works for them," she says.

- **Be helpful.** The experts advise making yourself as useful as possible tidying up, doing laundry, making meals, and serving as the family photographer. "But always ask permission first," warns first-time grandma Joanie K. "You don't want to give the impression that the new mother's housekeeping isn't up to your standards. Then, too, when you go shopping for the baby, always ask the mother first and, though it's tempting, don't buy out the store. You don't want it to look like you're taking over."

- **Be the babysitter.** If you get to babysit and your son gives you detailed instructions, just smile and say, "Great!" Never mind that you raised four children and are a registered nurse—in the neonatal unit no less. Chrissy C. is proud that she and her husband were the twins' first babysitters. She could tell the new parents were nervous about going out, though, so she sent them texts throughout the night showing the babies eating and sleeping.

- **Be agreeable.** Go along with all the new parents' choices, no matter how off-the-walls they seem to you. They don't want the baby to drive with Grandpa? Take an Uber. They worry that visitors transmit germs? Ostentatiously rub Purell on your hands and only kiss the baby on his feet or the back of his head. These early transactions are setting the stage for your role as a grandparent, and you want to be thought of as "the easy one."

- **Be calm.** Or at least appear calm. Calm is catching. Even with a fussy baby and a nervous new mother, you can help lower everyone's stress level by seeming to take it all in stride. Think back to what worked with your own babies: walking them around, bouncing them on your knee, singing, talking, stroking. Don't remember? Go online, read a book, or take a grandparenting class.

- **Be understanding.** When the new mom has the blues, you want to provide a nonjudgmental shoulder for her to lean on. "Think of yourself as her cheerleader," says Barbara N. "Remember how scary it was to be responsible for a tiny, helpless human being who can't tell you what's bothering them?" According to the experts your new favorite phrases should be, "You're doing a great job!" and "I'm so proud of you!" Don't give unsolicited advice or recount how you did it.

- **Be conciliatory.** As soon as you hear that the kids are expecting, reach out to the other grandparents, coordinate visits, and stay in touch. After all, who else is going to find 64 ultrasounds of a uterus fascinating? Now is also a good time to make peace with your ex, if you have one. You'll be sharing your grandchildren's big occasions, and it will be a relief to the new parents to know there won't be awkwardness or acrimony when you're all together.

- **Be responsive.** "Our son was never one to call unless he had a specific topic to discuss," says Joanie K. "Now he's a regular Chatty Cathy, narrating videos of his baby daughter almost every day. We make sure to get right back to him so he knows we're with him all the way."

- **Be impervious to irritations.** "My daughter-in-law is a complainer and she does things in a way I wouldn't," says Chrissy C. "But when I held the babies in my arms for the first time, nothing else mattered—and six months later, it still doesn't."

To Go or Not to Go?

Walter is a widower whose grown daughter, Dawn, and son-in-law, Mike, think they're cheering him up by inviting him to every school play, soccer match, and tap recital in which his grandchildren take part. This is not Walter's idea of a big time, but he doesn't want to hurt Dawn and Mike's feelings.

- *Should Walter go whenever he's invited?*
- *Should he decline selectively and gracefully?*
- *Or should he proclaim a blanket policy of not attending any kiddie activities?*

The Panel Weighs In:

George: *Even though Walter feels he paid his dues with his own kids, he has to suck it up and show up for his grandkids. It's expected today.*

Marco: *I think Walter can bow out of some events in which his grandchildren have bit parts. He could play the "elderly" card.*

Sascha: *If he really hates these command performances, Walter should decline as a general policy. Dawn and Mike might even be relieved not to have to worry about whether he's enjoying himself or not.*

Evie: *Walter doesn't have to go to every kids' event, but he should look for ways to show the family he likes being with them, such as taking them to a baseball game, his favorite spectator sport. Otherwise, he might be seen as a grumpy old man.*

Grandma Showers

According to Donne Davis, founder of the GaGa Sisterhood, there is now a new rite of passage—grandma showers. The guests bring baby gear for the grandma-to-be so she'll have all the stuff she needs when the baby comes to visit. Donne says she loves the idea of a grandma-to-be sitting in a circle of wise, supportive peers who want to help her celebrate her exciting new status. She envisions seasoned grandmas sharing what they've learned—and sometimes learned the hard way.

Donne says, "New grandmas can always use words of wisdom. They are often so infatuated with their new grandchild they forget the most important people in this new relationship: the grandchild's parents. Newbie grandmas are thinking "I can't wait to get my hands on that baby and smother him with kisses." What they should also be thinking is: 'How can I best support my adult children in their new parenting roles so that we can all feel like a cohesive team?'"

A rite of passage

Donne also advocates creating a rite of passage for new grandparents as a way to celebrate the start of this thrilling, new chapter in their lives. Some ideas you might consider are:

- Reminiscing with your spouse about your grandparents and envisioning how you'll be like and unlike them.

- Planting a tree to mark the day of the baby's birth. What a beautiful living reminder of your family's expansion.

- Visiting a sacred spot and contemplating the transformative power of grandparental love.

- Writing a commemorative poem, shooting a photo montage, making a philanthropic donation, or serving a festive family dinner.

- Sending a letter to the baby to be opened on his/her 21st birthday. The letter could describe your feelings about the birth, your hopes for the child's future, and a description of you and the values you want to see carried forward.

The Evil Step-Grandmother

Edie, a second wife, didn't have any children of her own, which was always a sadness for her. That's why, when her step-daughter, Dominique, gave birth to a boy, Edie was over the moon. Even if she had missed out on being a mother, she thought, at least now she would have the joy of being a grandmother. Unfortunately, Dominique had always resented Edie for getting between her parents, even though they had divorced well before her father met her. Now, Dominique is getting her revenge by withholding her child, making it clear that her own mother is the "real" grandmother and Edie has no role to play in the boy's life.

- *Should Edie suffer in silence?*
- *Should she confront her husband about his daughter's behavior?*
- *Should she insist on going to Dominique's house when he is invited but she is not?*
- *Should she try to enlist help from the other grandmother?*

The Panel Weighs In:

Sarah. Edie should talk with Dominique directly and tell her in no uncertain terms that genetics have nothing to do with loving, and a child needs all the family he can get. Dominique should be ashamed of herself!

Karen. Edie should lay out the situation for her husband, who does not get a pass here. He's got to step up and support his wife. If he doesn't, I fear for their marriage.

James. Edie has to back off and hope that Dominique will come around—probably when she wants some free babysitting. Offering to help is definitely the way to go.

Teddy. Edie has to "own" her role as grandmother. If she's confident that, of course, she will be a full member of the extended family, I think Dominique will fold. Going to the other grandmother is the world's worst idea. Either Dominique will feel bullied or she and her mother will close ranks against Edie.

Readers' Comments

Edie should find local hospitals that need volunteers to hold babies whose mothers took drugs. Please let this go and travel with your husband and ignore the rest. Detach. B.Z.

Dominique seems to be protecting her mother, who may be demanding this, or Dominique is still bitter that her parents have separated. Perhaps Edie could send a note reminding Dominique that every child deserves as much love and support the world can offer. She could let Dominique know that she has no desire to take her mother's place, but that she has heart is full of love for the grandson as well as for Dominique, and she is there for them. If Dominique still refuses, I hope Edie understands that this may not be personal. D.O.

What Is Your Grandparenting Style?

". . . Grandmother, as she gets older, is not fading but rather becoming more concentrated."

Paulette Bates Alden

Grandparents come in all sizes and shape—and degrees of enthusiasm for the job. Anecdotally, it seems that some new grandparents, especially women in their fifties, dread the title, which they say, "Sounds so OLD!" Perhaps that's why they come up with every nickname under the sun to avoid being called Grandma. Still, for everyone who says, "Don't count on me to babysit!" or "I have my own life to lead!" there seem to be thousands who can't wait to get their hands on that little bundle of joy.

Today there are no accepted norms for good grand-parenting. Even more than the parent/adult child relation-ship, it's very individual and voluntary. On the one hand, studies show that the grandparent role looms larger for the less educated, those who are older, unemployed, retired, or widowed, and those not involved in organized activities. On the other hand, grandparents with greater resources can help out the grandkids financially, give them new experiences, and travel long distances to be with them.

"Grandma always made you feel she had been waiting to see just you all day and now the day was complete."

Marcy DeMaree

On opposite sides of the spectrum are the remote individual, who shows up (or is called in) for milestone occasions, and the highly involved individual who either has regular, scheduled caretaker responsibilities or drops everything to babysit when called. There's also the so-called "fun seeker," who primarily provides entertainment for the grandchildren. Finally, there's the surrogate parent who has to take over the caretaking role when his/her children are unable to do so. This is called a "skip generation family," and it represents 2.7 million grandparents.

Formal and informal styles

Many factors contribute to your personal grandparenting style. If you're on the younger end of the spectrum, you're probably more informal in your dealings with the grandkids. Indeed, in my lifetime we've gone from "Grandma Smith" to "Grandma Joan" to, in many cases, just "Joan."

The old model of respect and obedience for one's elders went out many years ago when the experts told grandparents not to discipline but to cuddle, not to speak authoritatively but rather to listen sympathetically. Along the way grandparents were relegated to the periphery of their grandchildren's lives. Contributing to the diminution of their role was the fear of being considered "meddlers." So, rather than transmit their decades of hard-won wisdom, they zipped it, and younger generations lost out on much cultural and personal lore.

There are other forces at work as well! If you live far away, it's harder to make it work. AARP found that an overwhelming percentage of grandparents wish they saw their grandchildren more, but only a third lived within 25 miles of them. If the parents are not pro-active—or worse, have posted a "Grandparents Keep Out" sign, it's almost impossible to establish close bonds. If you're working or have a busy lifestyle, it's difficult to mesh schedules. Finally, with young people having children later, many grandparents are older and simply can't be as physical with the kids as they would like.

> *"If nothing is going well, call your grandmother."*
> Italian proverb

Evolving relationships

As your grandchildren evolve, your grandparenting style evolves with them. The kids might not climb onto your lap anymore, but many grandparents report that their new, grownup relationship with the grandchildren is even more gratifying than when the children were young.

> *"She's the one who taught me about hard work. She's the one who put off buying a new car or a new dress for herself so that I could have a better life. She poured everything she had into me."*
> Barack Obama on his grandmother
> Madelyn Dunham

No matter what your grandparenting style, or constraints, I urge you not to get into competitive grandparenting. Don't feel guilty if you are not whisking the whole family away to Hawaii for Christmas. Don't compare yourself to the Joneses who fly across country once a month to babysit. And don't fret if the Browns go to every one of their grandkids' soccer games and you don't. No matter what it looks like, the grandchild/grandparent relationship is second only to the parent/child relationship in importance. For those who of you who assume the mantle—at whatever level, in whatever way—know that you are making a meaningful, lifelong impact on your grandchildren.

Standing On the Shore

by Linda Schwartz

my grandson
stands at pond's edge
holding his parents' hands
traits of each reflected in his face
tossed pebbles skim the pond's surface
transforming placid waters
into ripple   after ripple   after ripple
lulling waves on an outward journey
blending generation to generation   father to son
mother to daughter   grandchild to grandparent
continuity of family   customs   traditions
washing gently on pond's sandy shore
to greet a waiting
child

Linda Schwartz is the author of Reflections: Poems about Life, Relationships, and Family.

The Bank of Grandma and Grandpa

The phrase "generous to a fault" certainly applies to America's grandparents. AARP reported that over a third of grandparents say they spoil their grandchildren by "buying them too much." And the aggregate spending on grandchildren is now over seven billion dollars a year and climbing fast. Part of the reason for this largesse is the wealth of baby boomers. They are better off than earlier generations so they have the wherewithal to make significant gifts, and their recipients of choice are often the grandchildren.

Helping out

Holidays and birthdays are the usual occasions for transferring cash, but surveys show that over half of all grandparents also help out with tuition and school supplies and over a third pitch in to defray day-to-day living expenses. Sandra Timmerman of the MetLife Mature Market Institute says, "[Grandparents] are not interested in holding back and saving the gifts for inheritances. They'd rather give smaller gifts now and see the fruits of their labor being used." MetLife found that only 21 percent of boomer grandparents specify gifts to the grandchildren in their will.

As the grandchildren get older, their expenses get greater. Unsurprisingly, their parents welcome all the help they can get thanks to the soaring cost of higher education. College costs have risen 120 percent in recent decades, leaving many parents—who may still be paying off their own student loans—with nowhere else to turn but the grandparents. Fidelity Investments found that more than half of all grandparents who earn high five figures or more already do or plan to start saving to help put their grandkids through college. And you can forget the $100 U.S. savings bond gift to a graduate. Nowadays, grandparents expect to contribute a median $25,000 and many are putting away $50,000 or more.

If you, too, want to help out your grandchildren, there are basically three ways to do it. The first is an outright gift of up to $15,000 ($30,000 for a married couple) without paying a gift tax. According to the IRS if you write a big check, gift some investments or give a car to someone other than your spouse or dependent, you have made a gift. The IRS has a gift tax limit, both for the amount you can give each year and for what you can give over the course of your life. If you go over those limits, you will have to pay a tax on the amount of gifts that exceed them.

Money for college

The second is setting up the qualified tuition plan know as a "529." Sponsored by states, state agencies, or educational institutions, these college savings plans are a form of mutual funds in which earnings grow tax-deferred and withdrawals are free from federal taxes if they're used for higher education. However, if you pull money out of a 529 for anything other than college, the earnings will be taxed as ordinary income plus a 10 percent penalty.

Finally, you can set up a custodial account. This money doesn't have to be used for college tuition, but the experts suggest you confine it to that. There are no tax breaks on a custodial account and, when your grandchild reaches his majority (defined by his/her state as 18 or 21), the money belongs solely to him. Alas, some grandparents get a nasty shock when they find out that some of their hard-earned money has gone toward a spring break getaway to Ft. Lauderdale! As valuable as the above-mentioned accounts are, be aware that they can sharply reduce your grandchild's financial aid, since that money is counted as an asset when applying for loans and grants.

Richard Eisenberg, author of *How to Avoid a Mid-Life Financial Crisis*, further advises, "If you do want to put money away for your grandchild's future college bills, I'd suggest setting up an automatic program that funnels the same amount from your checking account into the 529 or custodial account every month. This way you won't need to remember to make the gifts and you'll likely find it easier to part with the cash in dribs and drabs than by writing a giant check once a year or so."

Good saving habits

Finally, when gifting grandchildren the experts say it's best to specify the way the money should be used or make the purchase or payment yourself. Above all, they caution, don't bail the kids out of debt. That might just encourage them to keep spending, secure in the knowledge that you're there to backstop them. Instead, talk with your grandkids about developing the saving and spending habits that will stand them in good stead throughout their lives. Giving them the benefit of your experience might be the most valuable gift of all. Unfortunately, says MetLife's Sandra Timmerman, "We've found it easier for grandparents to give money than to give advice."

Alienated Grandparents

I get many heartbreaking emails detailing the callous treatment of a grandparent by a difficult daughter-in-law (DDIL). Here is a typical message from a Texas woman I'll call Doreen. Doreen wrote:

"I had a loving relationship with my granddaughters for a decade, although their mother was putting more and more restrictions on my interactions with them. She kept piling up the do's and don'ts—I eventually counted fifty of them—and they became more and more bizarre. At first I could visit and bring gifts. Over time she nixed the visits, but I could call and Skype. Then I couldn't call but I could write. Then I couldn't visit and couldn't write but could send gifts. Then I had to stop wrapping the gifts so she could see what was inside, then the gifts had to be sent to her so she could approve them first, and then I wasn't allowed to send gifts at all. Never was a reason given for these humiliations or finally shutting me out altogether."

Doreen reaches out

She continues, "I don't live near the children, but I made the effort to get to their home two to three times a year. I existed for these visits, our phone calls, and our Skype sessions. We had a loving relationship and now, after ten years of being a grandma, I have nothing. This is not estrangement, it is alienation. It's a form of elder abuse and child abuse.

"It's also a form of spousal abuse. My daughter-in-law has turned my kind, loving son against me. He was an Eagle Scout, for goodness sakes! But over time he bought into her lies and now he won't have anything to do with me. When I tried to meet him at a coffee shop recently, he turned me down cold. 'What part of 'no' don't you understand?' he said. "And if you try to come here again, I'll get a restraining order against you," which he did. It's a nightmare that never ends. Does this younger generation have no feelings for anyone but themselves?"

A grandparent fights back

Given this kind of treatment, most grandparents give up. The constant rejection is just too painful. But Doreen says grandchildren are worth fighting for, both for your sake and theirs. Here's what this feisty lady recommends:

- **Send postcards**. This way the parents can see what you're saying. The message should be neutral, something along the lines of "Grandma is thinking of you." The kids have got to be able to trust love, she says, even if the parents are setting a terrible example.

- **Keep trying to communicate**. Your phone calls may go unanswered, but one day there may be a breakthrough. And, if you get to leave a message, the kids may hear your voice.

- **Keep trying to visit**. Doreen urges other grandparents to go in person, but she says to take someone with you to witness the exchange. Also, it may be less threatening—and the parents may behave better—if there are two or three of you.

- **Go to the police**. If, God forbid, the parents put a restraining order on you as Doreen's did, she says you should go to the police yourself to explain what's going on. When they hear your side of the story, they may be able to help. In her case, they agreed that dropping off a gift for the grandchildren was not harassment but a domestic dispute, and they recommended that she see them first if she tries to visit again. Then they thanked her for coming in. "We drive by these beautiful homes," one told her, "but we don't really know what's going on inside."

- **Reach out to their minister**. Speak with your son and daughter-in-law's minister to apprise him or her of what's happening. Clergy may be able to help effect a reconciliation or at least try to get you invited to your grandchildren's milestone occasions from which you might otherwise be excluded.

- **Join a support group**. Whether online or in-person, these groups can provide moral support, information, and expert advice. Doreen found it comforting to learn that hers was not a unique situation.

- **Advocate on a larger scale**. Doreen alerted me to Alienated Grandparents Anonymous, which lobbies locally, nationally, and internationally for greater awareness and legal protection for grandparents. See the next article for a fuller explanation of what AGA does.

Resources for Alienated Grandparents

Grandparental estrangement is an international epidemic—in Ontario, Canada, alone a reported 75,000 grandparents cannot see their grandchildren—but at least it's an epidemic that is finally coming out of the shadows. Grandparents are banding together and, like Doreen in "Alienated Grandparents," they're fighting back. They are forming info-sharing organizations, joining online support groups, and advocating on the state and national level for legal standing. Here is a small sample of their activities:

Alienated Grandparents Anonymous. Headquartered in Naples, FL, and with members in every state, AGA offers free meetings, a national conference, YouTube presentations, tips from experts, and online outreach that provides information and support. It stresses reunification and reconciliation for families and lobbies for state laws that include consideration of grandparents among divorcing couples and intact families. Their brochure claims, "Studies show that the best form of help for complicated grief (grief without closure) is a peer-led support group." *www. AGA-FL.org.*

Grandparent Rights Advocates National Delegation of the United States of America. This is an organization dedicated to the development and/ or modification of legislation providing legal recourse for grandparents denied visitation with their grandchildren. Grand-USA is committed to the children, their alienated grandparents, and the survival of extended families in all fifty states. They have state affiliates and urge those interested to join the grassroots effort to create and amend legislation for grandchildren and grandparents to help them remain connected. *www.grand-usa.org.*

Facebook Groups. When you log into Facebook, you can will find several groups that speak to the crisis in extended family relations today. Among them are Grandparent Alienation 101, Grandparent/Grandchild, Estrangement/Alienation is not Natural, Find my Grandparent, and Grandparents without Grandchildren. Their memberships are surprisingly large—and growing fast. What a boon to have these resources available to grandparents day or night right from their home.

Grandparent Alienation Awareness Day. For the past three years many states have declared a day in mid-June Grandparent Alienation Awareness Day. Activists use this day to put their case before judges, lawyers, state legislators, advice columnists, mental health practitioners, MD's, and teachers. Several of the states observing Grandparent Alienation Day are not the ones you would expect, including Texas, Kansas, and Virginia. Here is part of the proclamation from the governor of Alabama:

- WHEREAS, alienation is a term used to describe any number of behaviors and attitudes on the part of one or both parents, designed to interfere, damage or destroy the relationship between a child and family member. It is a form of abuse that causes emotional trauma to children; and

- WHEREAS, alienation behaviors are frequently present in high-conflict divorces, separations, asymmetrical custody arrangements, and in intact marriages, often causing mental and emotional anguish to children; and

- WHEREAS, mental health professionals agree that the negative effects of alienation can follow a child into adulthood with tragic consequences; and

- WHEREAS, Grandparent Alienation Awareness Day is intended to increase the knowledge and understanding of this problem to help families, institutions, the legal and mental health community, and leaders to better identify and combat such abusive behavior to children:

- NOW, THEREFORE, I, Kay Ivey, Governor of Alabama, do hereby proclaim June 14, 2017, as **Grandparent Alienation Awareness Day**.

Going Directly to the Grandchildren

Tom wants to have a one-on-one relationship with his teenage grandchildren, but Tom's son Vic, insists on being present. Vic seems to be afraid that either Tom will give his children advice that's contrary to his wishes or the kids will give away family secrets. Tom doesn't want to alienate his son, but he longs for a direct connection with his grandchildren without Vic continually running interference.

- Should Tom have a heart-to-heart with his son?
- Call the kids when Vic is at work?
- Accede to his son's wishes?

The Panel Weighs In:

Vince: Tom has to be straight up with his son. A relationship only works when one person doesn't always feel he's compromising.

Melissa: These are Vic's children and Tom has to do it Vic's way as long as they live at home. They'll be in college soon and then he can call them directly.

Chuck: Tom is between a rock and a hard place here, either turning off his son or settling for a less-than-satisfactory relationship with the grandchildren. It's the better part of wisdom to maintain the status quo.

Lee Ann: There's always letter writing, texting and emailing. It might be a one-way street flowing from grandparent to grandchildren, but it's worth a try.

The Double-Edged Nature of Being a Grandma

by Donne Davis

"Tell me a story about your grandma," my 11-year old granddaughter asked during a recent visit. "Well, you know you're named after her," I said, "She was my best friend when I was growing up, and I loved spending the night at her apartment."

A grandma's stories

My grandma Amelia was a playful storyteller who was devoted to my parents and my two brothers and me. She loved to play cards with her circle of friends and traveled around the world three times with my grandpa. But she was a homebody at heart. A second-generation San Franciscan, she shared her stories of camping out in Golden Gate Park as a 12-year-old after the great 1906 earthquake.

I can still picture her corner apartment in the San Francisco Richmond district. When my grandpa was alive, I slept on their davenport in the living room right beside the radiator which hissed in the morning when it first came on. After he died, I slept in his twin bed beside my grandma.

I could hardly wait until Saturday to go on one of our outings. My grandma and I took the 38 Geary bus downtown dressed in suits and white gloves. We admired the window displays in the City of Paris, I. Magnin and Macy's in Union Square then walked down to Woolworth's Five and Dime for lunch at the counter. We ordered "all-around strawberry sodas" and happily slurped up the last drops through our straws. Sometimes we took the cable car and walked through Chinatown then slipped inside Old St. Mary's Church to light a votive candle on the altar.

My favorite outing was a Saturday matinee at the 4-Star theater on Clement Street. Before we saw the movie, my grandma gave me a dime to spend at the penny candy store across the street. My dime bought me 20 pieces of candy.

An inherited sweet tooth

Our trip to the penny candy store is my granddaughter's favorite story. She has a sweet tooth just like my grandma and can't believe I could get 20 pieces of candy for a dime. "When I'm a grandma," she said, "I'm going to tell my grandchildren about you, Baba." I thought of my grandma and how pleased she'd be to know her namesake has a fondness for sharing family stories. Later, I told my daughter of Amelia's sweet pledge and teared up knowing I would not be around to meet her grandchildren.

That's the "double-edged nature of being a grandma" writes Robin Marantz Henig in her poignant *New York Times* essay: "The Agony and the Ecstasy of Grandmother-hood." "Your thoughts turn powerfully toward the future— one that now includes the grandchildren you adore—at the very same moment you're reminded of your own absence from that future. It's an odd mixture of birth and death, which is what gives grandmotherhood its beauty, as well as its specific and poignant pain."

Having recently lost my husband, I'm experiencing that paradox first hand. As I watch my granddaughters without their beloved grandpa to witness all their joyous celebra-tions, I'm aware of my own mortality more than ever before. Though my joy is bittersweet, I cherish the precious moments that I do get to share with them even more.

Donne Davis is the founder of GaGa Sisterhood and author of When Being a Grandma Isn't So Grand: 4 Keys to L.O.V.E. Your Grandchild's Parents.

When Your Children Won't Be Having Children, Part 1: Dashed Expectations

When family size shrinks, it is one thing, but when it disappears altogether, it leaves many parents of grown offspring feeling incredibly sad because they will never have grandchildren. The reasons couples today are not starting families are all over the map: They can't have children, they don't want children, they married too late to have children. The couple is gay. The daughter never married. The wife is infertile and in vitro didn't take. They have horrendous student debt, they can only afford a tiny apartment, the job market is unstable, they are discouraged about the world. In addition, some young people have had serious medical issues and don't want to risk a pregnancy, some are concerned about their family's faulty gene pool, and others are nervous about or even anti adoption. Still others, very frankly, don't want to give up their metropolitan/frequent flier lifestyle.

Attitudes are Changing

Perhaps the most important factor of all, though, is the changing attitude in our society toward not having a family. It's now okay to say you're enjoying your childless state, a sentiment that would not have been acceptable years ago. "In the past women had children because that was what was expected of them," says natural health specialist Dr. Eva Detko. "Women today have more options and they don't feel the same societal pressure to marry young and reproduce early and often."

Hopeful grandparents cannot take heart from demographic projections, either. The Pew Research Center estimates that as many as a quarter of millennials may never have children. Stewart D. Friedman, a professor at the University of Pennsylvania's Wharton School of Business and author of Baby Bust: New Choices for Men and Women in Work and Family concurs. His research shows that in 1992, 78 per cent of graduating students from the U. of P. said they planned to have children. In 2012 only 42 per cent did—a decline of nearly half in just 20 years—and these figures were nearly identical for both sexes.

Parents left with a sadness

"Having grandchildren wasn't so much an expectation as an assumption," Bonnie K. told me. "But then life has turned out very differently for us Baby Boomers than for our parents, hasn't it?" Don N. mused, "You're meant to go through certain experiences at certain points. Without grandchildren, I feel I'm out of sync with life." Other comments I heard were: "I can only describe it as an empty feeling," "I was devastated," and "I loved being a mother and I was so excited by the thought of becoming a grandmother. It's the next step—but it doesn't look like I'm going to be taking it."

The parents I spoke with didn't blame their adult children, whom they felt had the right not to reproduce if that's what they wanted. Still . . . "I knew I was making my mother happy when I had a child," said Dawn W. "It wouldn't even enter my daughter's mind to make us happy. I know she loves us, but she is fulfilled by having a dog." For some people the sense of loss didn't set in right away. Dinah P. confided, "I was so happy when my son found this wonderful woman that I didn't care about the abstraction of babies. But now when I see other peoples' adorable grandkids, I yearn for them. I also see how wonderful it would be to have another person who loves you beyond your husband and your friends." It was not originally a sadness for Lisa M., either, who was so into her daughter that she never thought about having another child. "Now," she says ruefully, "I would buy one if it meant I could have grandchildren." Jerry Q. was blue about that the fact that, "This is the end of the line for my line." Maureen G.'s biological clock had run out for herself, but she held out hope for her stepchildren. "At least your kids will have our grandkids," she said to her second husband. But they didn't.

New grandparents are insensitive

The parents I spoke with claimed their feeling of missing out on something special has been exacerbated by the insensitivity of others. New grandparents are the worst, apparently, indulging in what has been termed "grandparent triumphalism." This leaves non-grandparents feeling left out. "It's like a sorority that I wasn't asked to join," said Linda C. "I stay away from them as much as I can." Karen B. said of some professional grandparents, "They're the ones who didn't have much of a life before and this is their big moment." By their over-the-top participation in—and recitation of—the younger family's lives, these exuberant grandparents rub salt into the wound, feeding "grandchild envy." As Kathy F. experienced it, "A member of our bridge group bragged so incessantly about her grandchildren that I finally couldn't take it anymore. There's a young girl I'm close to, so I began to brag about her just for something to say. I'm fighting back!"

Readers' Comments

I can honestly say that until my daughter, who has been a successful, world traveling businesswoman, married 5 years ago at 36 and had a baby at 40 by IVF, I was concerned that I might not have grandchildren. I had many of the feelings described above. I am now a happy grandma, thrilled to show photos and videos of my adorable grandson... always trying to be sure I don't offend anyone who may not have grandchildren of their own. The years are definitely passing, and I am grateful for this new addition to our lives. K.L.

This is a deeply painful subject for more of us than I thought. I had assumed that with three children, at least one would marry and have children, but this doesn't seem to be coming down the pike anytime soon and my daughters' biological clocks are running out. I echo all of the other sentiments above: a feeling of emptiness, envy, and exasperation at incessant grandparent talk among my peers. Yet, I cannot blame them; why should they hold back from discussing such a natural topic? Our children choosing to go childless is ominous and strange and it fills me with a sadness and somewhat of a lack of purpose, especially now that I'm retired. The years are passing. I try to build my life with a fitness routine, volunteer work, social activities, hobbies, etc. but there is something missing; a big something. I wish there were a support group for us. V.O.

When Your Children Won't Be Having Children, Part 2: Filling the Void

In the previous article, I looked at the impact of not having grandchildren. As one might expect, the parents who found themselves in this situation experienced sadness, emptiness, and even devastation. But most of the fathers and mothers I spoke with eventually found creative ways to cope. Here's how:

Some POGOs look at the glass half full

They value what they have rather than obsess over what they don't have, i.e. grandchildren. "I have so much more free time," said one. "I don't have the emotional entanglements a lot of my friends have due to bitter custody battles and their grandchildren's boring soccer games" said another. "I've got a lot more discretionary money," said a third. "So many of my friends have to pay for their grandchildren's private schools and camps, but I'm free to be philanthropic and also indulge myself in little ways before I go to that great bridge game in the sky."

Some parents double down on their relationship with their adult children. "I think my daughter and I talk to each other more and at a deeper level than we would if she had had children," said one woman. "It's simpler," said another. "Even if I had grandchildren, there's no guarantee we'd have precious, lifelong intimacy. But human beings do need an outlet for their love, so I'm pouring mine into my husband and our dog."

Some POGOs are surrogate grandparents

One POGO took over with the kids when his best friend died suddenly at the age of 42. With the friend's widow floundering, this man and his wife stepped in to provide stability and normality to the household. "The kids told us they liked us better than their real grandparents," he said, gloating only slightly. "In fact, they made up a certificate that declares us their honorary grandparents, so in a way, they adopted us. They were so needy after their father died, and I guess we were needy, too, without grandchildren. For years we had a weekly date with the kids—playing games, going to movies, ordering in for pizza—just the way we would if we were a real family. Fortunately, they also bonded with our grown children, so family occasions work out great."

Another couple became accidental surrogate grandparents when they sponsored a music student at a local conservatory. This young oboe player travels around the world for his work, but he takes it upon himself to visit his "grandparents" when he's within a two-hour drive of their home. One year he arranged a small concert for his surrogate grandfather's birthday. "We consider him our grandchild," said the wife, "so I guess you could say we moved up to pseudo-grandparenthood."

The accidental grandmother

The prize for the most unusual route to accidental grandparenthood must go to the woman who acquired a grandson when her gay son donated his sperm to lesbian friends who wanted to have a baby. Her son stayed in the picture and now she is considered the child's grandmother. "One of the lesbian mothers calls me "Nonnie," said the woman, "which is strange but nice. I can't say I feel that I'm a 100 percent grandmother, but as I age it's a blessing to have a connection with any youngster who can bring more love, light and 'connectedness' into my life."

Others are more deliberate in their quest

Some POGOs make a concerted effort to acquire grandchildren in untraditional ways. Their pro-active efforts include "adopting" nieces, nephews, neighborhood children, and dear friends' grandchildren. "Even though I'm just an 'honorary' and not the real deal," said one woman, "I still have the joy of hugging, holding, kissing, buying onesies, reading to the baby, showing pictures, and bragging about what a genius she is because she can hold her head up! A child can't have too many people who love her, and enlightened parents welcome the extra attention and help that an 'honorary' can bring."

Other would-be grandparents volunteer with family service agencies that match young families with seniors for mutual benefit. Others get trained to serve on the pediatric wards of local hospitals. Mothers' clubs are another source of young families who would welcome attention from a surrogate grandparent as is Parentless Parents, a support group with chapters in several states.

Online services help

Some seniors are taking advantage of new online services, such as Find-a-Grandparent in Australia, and Surrogate Grandparents in the United States. Surrogate Grandparents is a private Facebook group that works like Match.com to pair up seniors and young families. Surrogates and parents post profiles of themselves and then get acquainted through texts, emails, phone calls and, ultimately, face-to-face visits. When the relationship clicks, it fills a yawning void for all concerned. "Even though our adoptees live far away," said one surrogate grandfather, "we make it work by sending one another little gifts, exchanging cards, and celebrating the big holidays together. Teaching our adopted grandson to fish was the kick of a lifetime for me," he said.

Fortunately, today's extended family can come in all sizes, shapes, and configurations, including biological and adopted. Those seniors who really want to have a special relationship with a child now have more avenues open to them than ever before.

Chapter 3

Mothers and Daughters, Fathers and Sons

In this chapter I write about the linkages between core family members who are of the same sex but of different generations. These relationships may be many things, but uncomplicated is not one of them. Whole tomes have been written about how women bond and how those very mechanisms that foster closeness can also foment dissension. Similarly, huge, scholarly works and popular novels focus on sons trying desperately to win their father's approval, only to meet with rejection.

Part of the competition and conflict, according to pioneering psychoanalysts, stems from children's yearning for their parent of the opposite sex. The ancient Greeks, who had great insight into the human heart, gave us Oedipus, the king who accidentally kills his father and marries his mother. The Greeks also created the character of Electra, who helped plot the death of her mother to avenge her father's murder.

Sigmund Freud coined the phrase "Oedipus complex," when he described a boy's feelings of desire for his mother and jealousy and anger toward his father. Similarly, Carl Jung used the term "Electra complex," when he wrote about the corresponding feelings in which girls feel a desire for their father and jealousy toward their mother. Freud, went on to say healthy youngsters eventually resolve their conflicted feelings and identify with their same-sex parent.

Elvis and Gladys: A Love Story

Everyone loves their mother, but I was an only child and my mother was always right with me, all my life, and it wasn't just like losing a mother, it was like losing a friend, a companion, someone to talk to. I could wake her up any hour of the night and, if I was worried or troubled about something, she'd get up and try to help me."

Elvis Presley on his mother's passing

I love stories of filial devotion and this one tops the charts, as befits the King of Rock 'n Roll. Elvis Presley's twin brother was stillborn, which is often given as the reason why his mother, Gladys, kept him so very, very close. Although his father, Vernon, was very much in the picture, it was his mother who gave him his first guitar, found the money for a few lessons, and always encouraged his ambitions.

Showing his love

When Elvis hit it big at a very young age, he did his best to make up to Gladys for the deprivations they had both experienced. He set up Gladys Music, a publishing company from which she would get the royalties, and made good on his childhood promise to buy her a Cadillac—bright pink was his choice—even though she didn't know how to drive.

In the last years of her short life, Gladys was upset about the girls who threw themselves at her son's feet and depressed about his induction into the Army and deployment to Germany. By 1958 her health had deteriorated so significantly from hepatitis that she had to be admitted to the hospital, where she died at the age of

46. The Army had granted Elvis leave to come home, and he cried out at her grave, "Oh, God, everything I have is gone. Goodbye, darling, goodbye. I love you so much. You know how much I lived my whole life just for you." His fans grieved right along with him, sending more than 150,000 condolence cards, letters and telegrams and over 200 floral arrangements. In 1962 Elvis paid tribute to Gladys in song with "Mama," which can be found on YouTube.

Elvis buried his mother at Graceland, marking the grave with a tombstone that read, "Sunshine of our Home and Not Mine, But Thy Will Be Done." He followed her into death 19 years later, to be laid to rest at her side, where she always wanted him.

Playing Favorites

It's taboo in our society to admit that we favor one child over another. Yet when Cornell researcher Karl Pillemer interviewed older mothers in the Boston area about their adult offspring, he found, "Most mothers have very distinct preferences. There's one to whom they feel emotionally close, one with whom they have the most conflict. Parental favoritism is a fundamental part of the family landscape throughout life." Moreover, he contends, adult children are aware that their parents feel closer to one child than another. "They typically think it is themselves—and they're typically wrong," said Pilmer.

Closest to the mother

He says that what counts is who is emotionally closest to the mother, thinks the most like her, and shares her attitudes and values. Also, she (for it is usually a daughter) is the one who provided support for the mother in the past. Surprisingly, marital status, a poor employment record or even drug addiction doesn't seem to count in the "favorite child" sweepstakes.

Often the roots of favoritism go back to the earliest days of childhood. Parents may strive to love their children equally, but, according to psychotherapist Elizabeth Wolfson, PhD, "While we may love fully and differently, it is impossible to love equally. Of course, for kids that won't be enough. Each one wants to be the favorite, the special one." Experts say that children often perceive their place in the family in roughly one of three categories, self-definitions that may resonate throughout their lives.

The Favored One often grows up to be self-confident, but he also has to contend with a lot of pressure to live up to his parents' idealized version of him. He may become a habitual pleaser or find adult relationships wanting if they don't replicate his folks' 24/7 adulation.

The Overlooked One may suffer from what is often referred to as "middle child syndrome." She may nurse feelings of being ignored, leading her to act as the go-between in the family or clamor for the attention of the leader.

The Disfavored One may have low self-esteem and even depression throughout life based on his perceived black sheep status. He may become contentious and preemptively rejecting. On the other hand, since he thinks he has less to lose in his parents' eyes, he may feel liberated and take greater chances in life.

What to do about our children's self-assessment today? According to Dr. Wolfson, your adult children are entitled to their narrative, and you should resist the temptation to refute it. On the other hand, she says, you don't have to buy into it. Without dredging up all the old baggage, you might respond to their accusations of favoritism with such phrases as, "I'm sorry that hurt you" or "I didn't realize you felt that way." This gives you a way to express empathy without actually apologizing for things you may or may not have done in the dim, dark past. Sometimes it takes years, having children of their own, and/or lots of therapy for children to stop blaming their parents for playing favorites. But if you try to see your offspring as the grownups they have become and they try to see you as a mere mortal with feet of clay, you can all have a more satisfying relationship going forward.

Brain Chemistry Links Mothers and Daughters

That old saw, "A son is a son 'til he gets him a wife, but a daughter is a daughter all of her life," now has scientific underpinning. It's a dynamic and symbiotic relationship that transcends all others, according to a study published in the *Journal of Neuroscience*. Mother-daughter relationships are the strongest of all parent-child bonds when it comes to the common ways their brains process emotion. According to the 2016 study on 35 families, the part of the brain that regulates emotions is more similar between mothers and daughters than any other intergenerational pairing. Although the research base was small, other studies have explored this deep bond.

Empathetic connections

While the connections between mothers and sons, father and daughters or fathers and sons may be built on solid foundations of love, they aren't always as strong in the empathy departments. Based on the findings, brain chemistry is responsible for that.

That means mom is more likely to understand where you're coming from when faced with a problem because she could imagine herself in your shoes. (Or it could explain all the times you two have butted heads—the same sides of magnets repel each other, after all!)

The study also has potentially helpful implications when it comes to our understanding of mental health conditions. Lead author Fumiko Hoeft, an associate professor of psychiatry at the University of California, San Francisco, explained that the examined corticolimbic system is strongly tied to depression. That makes mothers' mental health experiences good predictors for their daughters. Considering there are good outcomes for preventative depression treatments, that knowledge of family history can be hugely helpful.

As the study was just the first to use intergenerational MRIs to compare brain structures, Hoeft hopes further research can explore the link with other mental health conditions in ways that could benefit all members of the family. In a press release, she said, "Anxiety, autism, schizophrenia, dyslexia, you name it—brain patterns inherited from both mothers and fathers have an impact on just about all of them."

Another study determined the connection between mothers and daughters remains stronger than other types of intergenerational family relationships throughout all the changes of life. Not surprisingly, more research has shown mothers and daughters influence each other—for better or worse—in different ways than other relationships.

Now we know that is both a matter of the heart and the brain.

My Grown Daughter/My Self

Some mothers and daughters are best friends, but many others have a prickly relationship, whether it's out in the open or just beneath the surface. Since avoiding conflict in the first place is almost always better than trying to repair a rupture, here are some pointers from the pros that can help you deal with the situation when you and your adult daughter seem to be moving in opposite directions.

Striving for independence

It's axiomatic—and healthy—that as an adult daughter strives for independence, she distances herself from her mother. But even mothers who understand why this is happening, and applaud it, may experience a sense of loss. Sadly, these feelings could cause a mother to fight too hard to keep her daughter close and in so doing achieve the opposite result.

According to Susan Adcox in *Verywell Family,* "The mother may ask questions that the daughter sees as intrusive, or give advice, which the daughter interprets as interfering. Deborah Tannen, the author of numerous books on family dynamics, writes, 'Given mothers' overactive improvement glands and daughters' overactive disapproval sensors, mother-daughter is a high-risk relationship.'"

The experts advise us to be supportive without being intrusive (not an easy thing to do) and show confidence in our daughter's life choices. We need to ask ourselves, while we dearly love the concept of "Mother knows best," do we always?

We are now aware, thanks to Tannen and others,

that women-to-women relationships are based on talking as opposed to men's relationships, which are more often based on doing. Tannen suggests that mothers take a leaf out of the men's book because talking can get us into trouble. As she says, "Women tend to talk more and talk about more personal topics, so this gives us more chance to say the wrong thing." Or else we don't listen. Or else we only like to tell our side of the story. If disagreements arise, psychologists advise, fall back on a shared activity or move on to a less personal topic.

Face-to-face

We are also told that women are better at communicating in person, where we can pick up on body language and other visible cues. When we have to communicate by phone, email, or text, we may experience more misunderstandings as well as a general loss of closeness. Still, if mothers and daughters live far from one another, we have to make the best of what we've got. When we can see each other through Skype or Facetime, for example, we still have the ability to gauge how our words are being received. The experts remind us to keep recalibrating our messages depending on what is sparking positive responses and what is going over like a lead balloon.

Those who have studied mother-daughter interactions endorse written communications, too, because they give both parties the opportunity to more carefully think out what they want to convey. On the other hand, written words can be misinterpreted as readily as spoken words, and they don't enable the writer to explain when her words are taken the wrong way. Moreover, emails and texts can live forever, as do the anger or annoyance they provoke.

Many mothers who miss the sound of their daughter's voice settle for texting, which is the main way younger people communicate. Other mothers connect with their grown daughters through social media platforms, such as Facebook. Whatever mode you choose, trading photos is considered a safe, popular, and benign way to stay in touch.

Although in most adult families, the mother is info central, the experts advise us to encourage direct communication among family members. As in a game of Telephone, the more the original message gets handed from person to person, the more it gets garbled. Moreover, if you're in charge of getting out the word, you might get blamed for favoring one daughter or daughter-in-law over another by telling her first. "Many women feel that closeness is the Holy Grail of relationships and knowing personal information is a sign of closeness," Deborah Tannen writes. Apparently, no one wants to feel left out or second best, least of all parents of grown children.

Porn In the Cabinet

Lily was babysitting her grandchildren while their parents, Sean and Missy, were on vacation. When she was looking for something to watch on TV, she stumbled across a large collection of pornographic videos in Sean's home office. Lily was shocked—her son had always been such a straight arrow. Moreover, she was concerned that her pre-teen grandchildren would find the tapes too. What should Lily do?

- Pretend she doesn't know anything about it lest Sean accuse her of snooping and bar her from seeing the grandchildren?
- Confront him and express her concerns?
- Try to find out what Missy knows?

The Panel Weighs In:

Dawn: Lily is snooping, pure and simple, and if she feels it's her place to confront Sean about his viewing habits, she's taking a big risk.

Cyndi: What's that stuff doing in the house in the first place!? Tell Sean in no uncertain terms, "This isn't how I raised you."

Joe: It's Sean's business what he wants to watch, but he's got to do a better job of keeping the porn where the kids can't get at it.

Gil: Sean and Missy are married, for God's sakes, and the porn tapes may be just what they need to spice up their sex life. Lily should butt out.

Michelle Obama's Mother

A True American Hero

After reading Michelle Obama's blockbuster memoir, *Becoming*, I concluded that her mother, Marian Shields Robinson, was the unsung hero of the Obama administration. Although reluctant at first to move into the White House—Michelle said she had to be strongly persuaded—Mrs. Robinson hung in for all eight years of the president's tenure, a reassuring presence for her daughter and a wonderful guardian for her granddaughters.

All those state occasions, all that digging in the vegetable garden, all that traveling on reelection campaigns—it's hard to believe Michelle could have done it had her mother not been on the premises and on the job with her two daughters. Of course, living in the White House had its glamorous upside for the "First Granny," but it also had the downside of leaving her lifelong friends and family in Chicago, where she was truly embedded. If the saying goes that behind every great man is a great woman, it could also be said that behind that behind many great working mothers is a truly great grandmother.

Mothers Who Are Jealous of Their Daughters

Normal or healthier mothers are proud of their children and want them to shine. But a narcissistic mother may perceive her daughter as a threat," claims Karyl McBride, PhD., author of *Will I Ever Be Good Enough? Healing the Daughters of Narcissistic Mothers.* "If attention is drawn away from the mother, the child suffers retaliation, put-downs, and punishments. The mother can be jealous of her daughter for many reasons: her looks, youth, material possessions, accomplishments, education, and relationship with the father, even her friendship with those who are closer to the mother's age than her own. This jealousy is particularly difficult for the daughter as it carries a double-message: 'Do well so that Mother is proud, but don't do too well or you will outshine her.'"

A mental health hazard

In fact, jealousy is crazy-making and creates huge barriers to the daughter's ability to create optimism and build self-esteem. What is the psychological benefit of jealousy? According to the experts, it allows an insecure mother to feel better about herself, at least for a while. When she criticizes and puts down her offspring, she reduces the threat to her own fragile self-esteem. Since mothers are often entering menopause when their daughters start to develop into desirable young women, it's often felt that it's normal for mothers to be touchy about their own declining desirability. However, Dr. McBride says that the poisonous envy felt by narcissistic mothers is anything but normal.

Narcissism plays a large role in this. While narcissists project grandiosity, the experts say they are actually self-loathing, fragile people who do not have a solid sense of self to rely on. They strike back hard, using name calling, making fun of people, putting others down, judging and being critical as a natural defense. The narcissist is just too insecure to do otherwise.

She acts out

"[The jealous mother] may be sarcastic, angry, give the silent treatment, or resort to personal attacks," says psychologist Nikki Martinez. "These are very impulsive reactions, and often [she] is not even aware of why she is behaving this way." But it leaves in its wake crippling self-doubt, intense insecurity, distrust, and hypervigilance. Since the narcissist is always wondering, "How does our family measure up to others?" their offspring spend a lifetime comparing themselves to others, as well.

If a mother is feeling jealous, she might want to one-up her daughter whenever the younger woman attempts to share some kind of success. "You can't mention that you are embarking on a new endeavor, taking a new class, updating your wardrobe, or signing up for a marathon without your mom following close behind," relationship expert Weena Cullin, LMFT, says. "Even if your motive isn't attention-seeking, a mom with jealousy issues will find it hard to allow you to grow without trying to stay on your level or one step ahead of you. This can knock the wind out of your sails, which is the intention," Cullin says. "Jealous moms have a difficult time responding to their children's accomplishments with genuine joy and happiness, so they just might try to steal yours."

Daughters Who Are Jealous of Their Mothers

Some say that young adult women today feel so competitive with their mothers that they should be called "Generation Jealous." These are the daughters struggling with their mothers' success or beauty or happy love life. As one journalist noted, "Even if there is no competition between the mother and the adult daughter, there is always comparison." And if the young women don't make the comparison themselves, friends and family will do it for them.

Daughters who are struggling

Of course, jealousy is more likely to rear its ugly head if the daughter is not happy with where she is in her own life. If she is finding it hard to make headway in the world, she may resent her mother's successful career. If she's over thirty and not married or involved in a significant relationship, she may resent her mother and father's strong bond. And if she is overweight or feels unattractive, she may resent her mother's good looks.

Given our society's obsession with physical beauty, it's no surprise that Internet forums on this topic are loaded with complaints from daughters who say their mothers are prettier than they. The younger women seem to particularly resent their mothers garnering more attention from men when the two of them are out together.

Writing in *Psychology Today*, Peg Streep, author of *Daughter Detox*, characterizes the accomplished mother as "The Oak." She says, "The Oak casts a long shadow over the sapling, and so the highly accomplished, sometimes witty and social, often beautiful and charming, mother makes it hard for her daughter to find her own place in the sun. In most cases, the daughter is very ambivalent. She's proud of her mom, on the one hand, and is pleased to note the ways in which she and her mother are alike; on the other hand, she also feels the need to differentiate herself from the mighty Oak and find an arena which is hers alone in which she can distinguish herself."

An international phenomenon

Daughter envy is not limited to the United States. In the British newspaper, The Telegraph, Radhika Sanghani wrote, "It's not always an easy road, following in your mum's footsteps—especially when she casts a long shadow." Sanghani quotes Linda Blair, a psychologist and author of *Happy Child*: "It's something I do hear a lot more than I used to," she says. "It's always been the case that daughters compare themselves to their mums but there weren't many [successful working] mothers until about 50 years ago. Now with the increased opportunities for women and the fact that we're so well for so long and we look great, it's true that young adult daughters find their mothers doing the same things they're doing, and of course they've been doing it for 20 or 30 years so they're ahead." As Blair concluded, it's a very different world today.

The Telegraph article cited the following examples to illustrate this point. "My mum and I are basically the same person, which can be difficult when you're trying to be yourself," says Laura, an executive assistant . . . And it's hard because I'm 26, I'm living at home, and she had a house at 21 and was married. I'm five years older than she was and I'm still playing catch up." Ling, 25, says: "I do feel as though my mum had achieved so much more than me by her mid-twenties—she had bought a house, had a good (well-paid) job, managed to settle down and was even pregnant with her first child. I'm renting in London, I'm on a junior salary and my boyfriend and I aren't thinking about marriage or anything right now. It's difficult because you constantly compare yourself to the people you admire and it seems as though our parents did everything so much younger."

Reader's Comment

I believe my daughter is jealous or envious of the relationship I have with the man in my life. I notice her being somewhat flirtatious and making a point to be around at the times she knows he will be home. She is always inquisitive as to where or what he is doing. She has a boyfriend but is not always happy in her relationship with him. L.W.

In the Closet?

Kyle's son, Jeff, has dated a few women over the years, but he's never seemed passionate about any of them. As Jeff nears 30, Kyle is wondering if his son is homosexual, asexual, or just "hasn't found the right one." Although they're not used to sharing intimacies, Kyle wants to assure his son that whatever his sexual orientation, he is 100% behind him.

- Should Kyle probe Jeff to see what's going on with his personal life?

- Should he invite Jeff to see a homosexual-themed movie or casually mention a same-sex married couple to gauge his son's reaction?

- What's riskier for their relationship, speaking up or not speaking up?

The Panel Weighs In:

Gene: *Although Kyle's bursting with curiosity, he has to keep mum and wait for Jeff to share.*

Jessie: *I disagree. If Jeff is pursuing an alternative lifestyle, it might be too hard for him to broach the subject with his dad. Kyle should get the ball rolling with some innocuous statement.*

Heidi: *Kyle is taking a big risk by plumbing his son's personal life. By aggressively pursuing the subject of his son's sexuality, Kyle could lose him.*

Melinda: *It's not an intimate father-son relationship now, so what's to fracture? Kyle's questioning could upset the status quo, but maybe that's a good thing.*

Presidents Are Parents, Too

When George W. Bush left office in 2009, he and his father could finally stop talking shop. The 41st and 43rd presidents were seen relaxing with each other in Texas and Maine, with no military aide hovering to deliver our country's nuclear codes in an instant. George H. and George W. simply shared the ordinary joys and sorrows of two aging family men. In their mutual post-presidency, George W. Bush seemed intent on making sure his father knew that he truly did admire him, painting a flattering portrait and writing what was called "an almost worshipful book" about his dad.

Growing up the eldest son of George Herbert Walker Bush wasn't easy. The younger Bush tried to walk the same path as his illustrious father, but he struggled with alcohol and had a wild streak. When he gave up alcohol after his fortieth birthday, George W. did spectacularly turn his life around, first as managing partner of the Texas Rangers and then as governor of Texas and president of the United States.

Jonathan Bush, brother of the elder Mr. Bush, said that although father and son were very close, his brother observed strict boundaries when George W. became president. "He was the perfect counselor because he would never give his advice. He would just listen," Jonathan Bush said in an interview.

When the end was near for his father, George W. knew he would not get back in time, so the two spoke via telephone. He told his father that he was a "wonderful dad" and that he loved him. In what were reported to be his last words, the father said, "I love you, too."

Making Men Out of Sons

Although we've come a long way from thinking the only real man is a Marlborough Man, many in our generation still have trouble embracing the full spectrum of manhood. Therein lies the rub between many fathers and sons. In addition to the problem of narcissism that afflicts some mothers, as we saw previously, fathers of grown offspring have to deal with leftover cultural stereotypes, boundary issues—if a son is named "Junior," isn't he supposed to be a mini-me?—and sometimes plain and simple jealousy: "Thanks to me, you've had it so easy compared to my early life. . ."

Jealous fathers

The website Quora posed the question, "Do fathers ever get jealous of their sons?" Alan Hall, who said he was "both a son and a father," responded about his own dad: "He put down, minimized, or actually made fun of every accomplishment I ever did. Sure, he would boast to all his friends about how great I was because that reflected well on him, but to me, it has been nothing but insults and put downs. His father criticized him too, so I have no doubt he was insecure about his abilities. Why he felt better by putting me down, I'll never know. I am very proud of everything my daughter does and I tell her that constantly.

"When I graduated with honors at USC with my MBA, he was resentful at all the attention I was getting. He told the whole family at the reception right after the ceremony: 'Sure, he has some "book" smarts. He is good at taking tests, but he doesn't have any "real" smarts, the kind that

I have, to make money! I am rich but he has nothing. He will be paying off his student loans for years. I could have paid for his college, but instead, I invested that money in a piece of real estate. In ten years, that property will be worth millions, and he will still be working his butt off in some cubicle, just another corporate slave. His education was the far worse investment. You will see.'

"I was the only one of his kids to go to college. I went on to a great career making 6 figures. I paid my loans off in 5 years. The piece of real estate he bought? He lost the entire $127,000 he invested when he allowed it to be foreclosed. The funny thing is, I advised him it was a bad investment to begin with. When a USC MBA gives you good advice, you should take it. LOL."

Fathers' expectations

When the son is gay, father-son relations get even trickier. Writing in *Psychology Today*, Ronald F. Levant, Ed.D. cited this example:

"In the Broadway play "Kinky Boots" the two lead actors are preoccupied with their struggles with their fathers' expectations. Charlie was the scion of four generations of shoemakers. His father expected that he would take over the business, which Charlie did not want to do. Simon grew up as a Black man in small town near London. His father wanted him to be a prize fighter like himself, and taught his son to box at an early age. But Simon had other ideas, and was more interested in being a drag queen, taking the name Lola. Charlie's and Lola's paths crossed while Charlie was being accosted and Lola stepped in to defend him, breaking the heel of her boot in the process. Charlie, being a shoemaker, offered to fix it, and in the process they formed a collaboration to make boots for men in drag—kinky boots. Together they sang "Not My Father's Son," in which the following lines expressed the dilemma they shared: "It was never easy/To be his type of man/To breathe freely/Was not in his plan/And the best part of me/ Is what he wouldn't see."

Dr. Levant attributes a lot of the angst to fathers' sense of obligation to create sons who are men in the classical/ traditional sense of stoic, aggressive, self-reliant, stay-calm-in-the-face-of-danger manhood. Fathers feel it is their job to wean sons of their neediness, and to put a hard shell around the children's vulnerable emotions, such as fear, sadness, hurt, and loneliness. The dads are constantly disappointed when the boys don't fit their rigid stereotype, which in turn breeds the anger, frustration, and low self-esteem that dogs them into adulthood. Dr. Levant concludes, "Parents need to be aware of the potential harm that could come from beliefs that the fathers' role is to make men out of their sons."

My Father's Hands

by Linda Schwartz

once rough and calloused from years of physical labor
his hands are now soft and pliant
mottled with bruises on tissue-thin skin

sitting by his bedside knowing his time is near
I whisper the Shema to him over and over
cover his hands with mine
unleashing a floodgate of memories

these are the hands
that held me as a newborn
but not again until three years later
a soldier returning home after proudly serving his country

these are the hands
that held the back of a wobbly two-wheeler
after training wheels came off
hands that built a tetherball set and a jungle gym
for our backyard

these are the steadfast hands
that linked mine as he walked me down the aisle
at my wedding
but trembled when he held
each of his newborn grandchildren

in the prime of his life
these hands packed a wallop of a serve in tennis
held fat Cuban cigars
cards for pinochle   gin rummy

and family penny poker

these are the hands
that lifted the Torah at his grandsons' Bar Mitzvahs
and passed it with pride
from generation to generation

for sixty-six years
these hands reached out to Mom lending support
as together they built a life   raised a family
these are the hands that embraced and held me
when I needed a father's comfort and love

his labored breathing is the only sound in the room
he can't hear me   he can't see me
I squeeze his hands firmly
letting him know I am by his side
hoping he can feel the depth
of love welling up inside me

in that dimly lit   silent room
I etch into memory every detail
every facet of his hands
take comfort in knowing
I will forever find solace and peace
in the sheltered memories
held in the harbor
of my father's hands

Linda Schwartz is the author of Reflections: Poems about Life,
Relationships, and Family.

Chapter 4

The Generation Gap

There are a ton of issues surrounding the younger generations, who are usually lumped together as "millennials" (just as older generations are lumped together as "boomers"):

- They're out of the house, and you're experiencing empty nest syndrome.
- They *were* out of the house, but now they're back.
- You're helping them out financially, and there's no end in sight.
- Their values are different.
- Their vocabulary is different.
- Their mode of communication (or lack thereof) is different.
- They may never marry, giving you grand-dogs instead of grandbabies.
- And they have tattoos, sometimes lots of tattoos.

In some ways it's the same old generation gap, but in other ways it's very different. Experts agree that adolescence is stretching out to encompass twenty-, thirty-, and sometimes even forty-somethings. Young people seem to be in no rush to get their driver's license, learn to cook or open a bank account, i.e., "adulting." They often act as if they are exceptional, but employers can find them entitled and poorly prepared for the workplace.

Today's parents may be unwittingly abetting this long adolescence by extreme involvement in their grown children's lives. Reports abound of "helicopter" or "snowplow" parents making sure their college students don't oversleep on exam day, picking out and furnishing apartments for recent grads, and even going on job interviews with them. Here are several articles to help you understand and better navigate the confusing world of our children and grandchildren.

Spendthrift Twenty-Something Child

G inny has tried everything to help her twenty-something son, Sam, live within his means. She has made out envelopes for his recurring bills, created an online budget that's easy to track, even offered to let him run his accounts through hers. Yet despite her best efforts, he consistently spends more than he makes, overages that she covers—and covers up with her husband, Paul—because Sam always seems to have some sort of plausible excuse for his expenditures.

- Should Ginny say "It's not my problem" and cut Sam off immediately, possibly jeopardizing her relationship with her son?
- Taper off the handouts?
- Make him repay what she's given him since college?
- Go into counseling for co-dependency?

The Panel Weighs In:

Rick: Ginny should be worried about jeopardizing her relationship with her husband by engaging in a cover-up rather than worrying about her relationship with her spendthrift son. Once she squares things with Paul, they both need to sit down with Sam and let him know that the situation cannot continue.

Julie: Ginny should insist on Sam's taking a personal budget workshop, which has the advantage of both cluing him in and taking her out of the equation. Clearly, Ginny needs to establish boundaries where her son is concerned.

Stu: She needs to taper off the handouts with a final cutoff in 3–6 months, and she has to follow through on this schedule. She also should insist that Sam repay her for everything she's laid out, starting now.

Laurie: Ginny should get a therapist for co-dependency and Sam should get a credit counselor for addictive spending. I would like to add that the kids' cell phone bills are a big issue in my family, too, and whoever invented the Family Plan should be shot!

Readers' Comments

Tough love is tough on the parents not the child, but as a parent you need to stop being an enabler. An enabler feels good but is very destructive to the child. Like birds, they have to try their wings. The time to stop is when they are physically able whether it is before or after college. You might be surprised that you really did raise a competent child. S.G.

It might be great to connect him with someone his own age who has a structured budget, savings, etc. plan. It's sometimes difficult for kids to take financial advice from their parents—particularly when there is a large income differential. It's easy for young people to fall into the "you can't possibly understand where I'm at" trap. OR "it's easy for you to talk about savings, you make/have so much more!" Advisement might be received differently (even if the advice is the same as the parent would give—don't we all know this paradigm too well?) when coming from a peer. P.N.

Tattoos: From Edgy to Everywhere

In 1975, there were only 40 tattoo artists in the country. By 1980, there were 5,000 and today there are 45,000 people plying the "skin mural" trade. Tattooing has become a multi-billion-dollar industry that's growing at the astounding rate of 13% a year! This remarkable phenomenon is occurring across all gender, age, and socio-economic lines as well as international borders.

Everybody's doing it

Once the province of sailors, gang members, and circus freaks, tattoos are now A-OK with suburban moms, doctors, attorneys, and even ministers. No matter what you might think of it, tattooing has undergone a rise in popularity that represents one of the most significant trends in Western culture. Since 20 percent of all Americans and 40 percent of all millennials have tattoos, don't be surprised if body art shows up one day in your family, too.

Tattoos go back thousands of years and evidence of them can be found in every part of the world. Whether as a rite of passage or a means of identification, tattoos were created in some tribal cultures by cutting designs into the skin and rubbing the resulting wound with ink, ashes or other agents. By contrast, modern tattoo artists use machines with electromagnetic coils that move an armature bar up and down. Connected to the armature bar is a needle that punctures the skin by about a millimeter and deposits a drop of insoluble ink with each puncture. The procedure is uncomfortable, but given the number of people who have it done again and again, the pain must not be unendurable.

Why did body art move from the underground and fringe crowds to the mainstream? Celebrities certainly had a good deal to do with it. Superstars such as Johnny Depp and Scarlett Johansson have not been shy about flaunting theirs, and soccer legend David Beckham proudly displays his 34 markings. As it has moved from counterculture to mainstream, tattoos can be seen on more parts of the body—fingers, ankles, necks, arms—and in ever more flamboyant colors and designs. They are considered a form of self-expression and as serious art. According to one psychologist who specializes in this area, "It seems to be predominantly about the idea that you feel unique as an individual. People get tattoos for all sorts of reasons but that's the underlying one."

Attitudes vary overseas

Not all countries are keen on body art, which is something to keep in mind if you are planning a family trip with tattooed relatives. In Japan, for example, tattoos are anathema because of their association with organized crime gangs, who pledge their allegiance with full-body markings. That's why even law-abiding citizens with tattoos are usually not allowed in public swimming pools, hot springs, beaches and even some gyms and general stores. North Korea bans religious tattoos and South Korea prohibits tattooing unless it is performed by a physician.

Some Christians object to tattooing based on Leviticus 19:28, which says, "You shall not make any cuttings in your flesh for the dead, nor tattoo any marks on you: I am the Lord." This is interpreted as God's desire to keep His people from engaging in pagan worship and sorcery. But one minister has postulated that Jesus himself may have had a tattoo, per Revelation19:16, "And He has on His robe and on His thigh a name written: KING OF KINGS AND LORD OF LORDS."

Orthodox Judaism, too, has a long history of distaste for tattoos, which are considered antithetical to the Jewish concept that our bodies are to be viewed as a precious gift on loan from God rather than our personal property to do with as we choose. However, the rabbis agree, there is no basis in Jewish law for refusing burial in a Jewish cemetery to a tattooed person, as is commonly believed.

Not universally admired

People considering getting a tattoo should bear in mind that while tattoos have attained widespread acceptance, numerous studies show that they can still put one at a disadvantage. Not only do employers and society at large still discriminate against tattooed people, but one study suggested that women with tattoos tended to be viewed as "less physically attractive, more sexually promiscuous, and heavier drinkers."

If you are of a generation that finds tattoos repellent, try to remember when your daughter, son or grandchild shows up with one that it's only skin deep. Besides, there's hope: the tattoo removal industry is also booming.

Goodbye to Their Childhood

by Marianne Bohr

It was only a month-and-a-half after our dark night in the depths of la France profonde—our deep embed in France. That night was the one and only time my husband, Joe, and I considered abandoning our European gap year to retreat stateside. But by the time our children, Chris and Caroline, arrived at Milan's Malpensa airport to join us for two weeks of our expat year, we had fully recovered our enthusiasm for the journey.

Their familiar American faces leapt from the airport crowd in full color as all others blurred to gray. From the moment they bustled through the international arrivals door, all was right with our world and I could barely control my excitement. I was jelly-kneed but on my toes, ready to pounce. There's nothing more beautiful than Caroline's smile and hearing Chris call me his pet name: "Maman!" The four of us converged in a "family hug," no one wanting to be the first to let go. Joe finally announced, "Guys, our Fiat awaits," to get us moving toward the exit.

Caroline asked, "How much Italian have you learned?" and I reminded her, "We've only been in Italy for three days, mia bella!"

Chris piped in, as he always did, "When do we eat?"

A very special time

Those two weeks with our children were bliss. We explored La Spezia, hiked the Cinqueterre, took silly pictures at Pisa, skied the Dolomites, and concluded our family trip in Verona. We stayed in a hotel appropriately named Giulietta e Romeo (give it a moment, you'll figure it out), dined at a trattoria with the same name, shopped at the open-air Christmas market, and snapped pictures at the mythical home of Juliet under its romantic balcony in a cobblestone courtyard. I did my best to enjoy the time, but as our sad parting loomed, I found myself sobbing in the shower on our last night in Italy, barely managing to pull myself together and dress for dinner tear-free, not wanting to ruin our final family evening.

The French have it right when they kiss and say au revoir—"Until we see each other again"—not "goodbye." And that's what we said to our children when they left us to go home. "We'll see you in less than four months, Dad," Caroline consoled Joe, but she was working as hard as he was not to cry. "Maman," Chris said, rubbing my back, "the next time we visit, you'll be in Paris. Just think about the meals!"

Joe and I both nodded and tried to smile, but it was time to say, "Until we see you again."

And so off they went, through security and to their gate, just four days before Christmas. While Chris's film-editing work was on hiatus for the rest of December, Caroline, a neonatal intensive care nurse, had to work through the holidays; otherwise, the kids would have stayed through Christmas Day. We yearned to board the plane with them, to remain in their company and head back to our familiar United States. But we busied ourselves with our own departure details and the mechanics of getting to another terminal to catch our EasyJet flight to London. The decision to leave for England on the heels of the kids' departure was a perfect foil for our melancholy. Distraction was a very helpful antidote.

Reality sets in

We settled in at our gate, and I did my best to lose myself in a book. But the chattering holiday travelers passing by made me feel the physical absence of the grown-up Chris and Caroline. I'd just hugged them goodbye so keenly that my face twitched and then crumbled, the tears I'd held back all day spilling over. Not only did I miss my adult children, as I realized in that moment, but I missed them as children as well. As happy as we are to see our sons and daughters grow, share the joy of their successes, help them deal with disappointment, and beam with pride as they become young adults, it's painful to say goodbye to their youth. Sitting on a molded plastic chair at a sterile airport gate, I miss my children's little selves—like friends I no longer saw—and I felt fleeting but unmistakable loss. I shared my thoughts with Joe and leaned my head on his shoulder. His voice thickening with sentiment. All he managed was, "I know, babe, I know."

The announcement of our flight to London interrupted my wistful reverie. I shook off my funk and strapped on my backpack, and we were on our way—stiff upper lip and all that. It was time for new adventures sans children; we were back to being on our own, back to being just two for the road.

Reader's Comment

I don't know whether to say sadly or gladly I have not felt such intense emotions when saying goodbye to my adult children after having an absolutely wonderful time with them.

And I can say with certainty that I have not experienced ever missing their little child selves. I have enjoyed every phase of development my children experienced (except maybe the sullen teen phase), but I don't miss any of them.

My favorite phase is now, whenever now is. I enjoy the adult to adult relationship with my children probably the most of any phase. I love the grown up, successful people they have become with their own opinions and ideas that don't always coincide with mine. And their own lives! Just as I have my own life. We have a warm, loving, caring relationship and enjoy each other's company, but they don't cry when I leave, and I don't cry when they leave. I know we will have many more good times together and that's nothing to cry about! S.D.

This article originally appeared in BoomerCafe.com as "Saying Goodbye." Marianne Bohr is the author of Gap Year Girl: A Baby Boomer Adventure Across 21 Countries.

Arf!

Jeannine's young adult son, Jamie, has a huge dog named Leo, whom he loves to pieces. Jeannine is expected to ooh and aah over the dog when she goes to Jamie's apartment, and then she is expected to babysit him in her home when her son travels for business, which is quite often. Jeannine can't stand Leo, who sheds all over her and her house, pulls her down the street when she's walking him, and never stops barking. Should Jeannine:

- Bite the bullet and suggest a trainer?
- Make up excuses for not babysitting Leo?
- Maintain the status quo in the interests of a good mother/son relationship?

The Panel Weighs In:

Gabriel: She should tell Jamie how she really feels about Leo and then bow out of the dog-sitting gig. If Jamie travels for business, he can afford to pay someone else to watch his dog.

Nanci: Jeannine should suffer in silence rather than jeopardize her precious relationship with her son. I'm sure Jamie is very appreciative of all she does for him. Besides, he may give her grandchildren one day.

Stefan: Just say no.

Bobbie: She should continue taking care of Leo but put a time limit on it. A day here or there is okay; one full week of having the dog in residence is not.

Empty Nest Syndrome

According to tradition, parents (especially mothers) are supposed to be extremely sad when their children leave home. They are said to feel an overwhelming sense of loss, loneliness, purposelessness, feelings of rejection, and worry about their offspring's welfare—in other words, the "Empty Nest Syndrome." From what I can see and have experienced myself, the Empty Nest Syndrome is indeed real. However, it doesn't seem to afflict every parent who is left behind, and its severity and duration vary widely even among those who do have it.

I know I panicked when my first child went to college, and she was only three hours away. Then two weeks later she was home to visit and drop off her dirty laundry, at which point I asked myself what had I been so upset about? Recently, I sat down with five mothers and one very involved father. Here is their first-hand testimony of what it was like for them when their children went off to college.

It was a blow

"I felt as though a lung had been removed from my body," says Kyla M. "I thought the worst was saying goodbye to my older daughter in her dorm, but the worst was actually seeing her empty room. That lasted a couple of weeks." Mal E. expected to be separated from her only child one day, but that day came three years sooner than planned. Her academically gifted son wanted to study German, which was not available at his high school but was a featured course at a prep school far from home. Sending him to boarding school at 15 was a wrench for Mal, to put it mildly. "After leaving him, I pulled off the road and sobbed," she says. "I didn't want him to feel my grief on top of all his other adjustments, so I held it in as long as I could. Letting him go away so young was a big sacrifice for me as a single mother, but I had made a vow at his birth that I was going to do everything possible for him or this whole motherhood thing wouldn't be worth it."

Elizabeth C. had time to get used to the idea that her daughter might go to school 3,000 miles away. Her husband took the girl on a tour of colleges during her junior year of high school, and it was clear that she was drawn to the East Coast, where the Chens have family and had visited regularly.

Elizabeth confesses, "She got into a good school and I was proud of her, but it was hard to let go. Of course, I was also sad when I dropped her off at kindergarten for the first time! I feel a real psychological connection to my daughter, and in the beginning I tried to maintain that connection through advice-giving, maybe too much so. I would ask, 'What classes are you taking, have you registered for them, are you getting together the docs for your student loan?' like a typical helicopter parent. After all, I had had input throughout her childhood and adolescence about what she needed to do, but once she got to college, she asserted her independence. I've chosen to feel not that she's rejecting me but that she's growing up."

Not everyone suffers

Unlike Kyla and Elizabeth, Julie M. was unaffected by the Empty Nest Syndrome. When I asked her how she felt when her twin sons went off to college, she replied unequivocally, "Great! I felt that my job as a parent was done." Her husband, Paul, who had been even more involved with the boys than she, said that he, too, was happy when they left for school. "I had wrung every bit I could from their childhood, including all the soccer matches, football practices, science projects, and camping trips known to man," he says. "I was done. Besides, there had been a progression toward independence every day since they could walk, so I felt confident that by the time they turned 18, they were ready to meet the challenges of their new lives. In the last year we discussed college so much that their actual going was a non-event. It was just time for all of us to move on."

Some young adults choose to stay home

But what if your child doesn't want to move on—is that even more disquieting? Bronwyn G. is frankly surprised that her son chose to attend college, albeit a prestigious one, in their hometown. He continued to live at home, for which she was grateful as it saved them a lot of money, but now, nine months after graduation, he's still there, working two part-time jobs.

"If he stays here, he won't be able to find the kind of programming position here that he studied for," she says, "but he doesn't seem to be looking very hard, either. I worry that I'm making it so comfortable for him at home he won't want to leave to better himself. Oh, well, I'm just going to have to take it as it comes because when I ask where he's applying for jobs, I get that 'Butt out, Mother!' look. He used to be an overachiever, having been voted president of his large high school twice, so I have to feel that one day he'll regain his old get-up-and-go. Then he'll fly the coop and I'll have Empty Nest Syndrome, only at a later age!"

Sink or Swim?

Dawn's son, Mark, is considering taking a job at a vitamin-supplement company. Mark is dazzled by the possibility of making a big pot of money through its pyramid sales operation. Something about the company didn't feel right to his mother, who investigated and found out it had a shady reputation. On the one hand, she's tempted to let Mark join them and learn a life lesson about making bad decisions. On the other hand, she fears he may unwittingly get drawn into something illegal that could dog him for the rest of his life.

- Should Dawn tell her son what she's learned and then back off?
- Should she keep mum to teach him to "look before you leap?"
- Is she obligated to warn him since something illegal might be going on?

The Panel Weighs In:

Alex: Even if the company does operate on the dark side, Mark will be too new and too far down the ladder for him to get into any real trouble if it goes south. I think learning about pyramid sales represent an invaluable opportunity for him no matter what, so Dawn should sit down and clam up.

Jackie: I disagree. Tough love sounds good in theory, but when your son's future is at stake, you have to do all you can to keep him from taking a serious misstep. Based on what she's learned, Dawn needs to throw *herself across the employment contract and shout, "No!"*

Kurt: *I think Dawn is obligated to share her intel with Mark. He sounds young and inexperienced and could use all the help he can get. If he decides to go ahead with the job anyway despite what Dawn's unearthed, at least her conscience will be clear that she did all she could to warn him.*

Diana: *Mark is an adult and should be treated like one. Dawn has to trust that her son is doing what's right for himself right now—and then she has to keep herself busy by keeping her fingers crossed that it will turn out alright.*

Readers' Comments

I once heard the expression about love. . . "L.O.V.E. is let others voluntarily evolve." While I think that is lovely, I also don't feel I could let my son walk into a situation like this without sharing some wisdom. E.R.

And your son may be receptive to that wisdom. In a 2015 study, recruiter Robert Half found that more than 80% of the university students surveyed said that their parents or guardians would influence their career choices. B.G.

I would share the information and then let it play out. I have recently dealt with the very same issue with my adult daughter. Fortunately, after I told her about some shady dealings at her prospective company (which she didn't believe) she found out on her own that they were true. I was tremendously relieved. C.B.

Shacking Up—Under Your Roof?

*C*huck Vaughn tells his parents he wants to come home *for spring break, and he wants to bring his girlfriend, Lindsay, with him. The Vaughns assume Chuck and Lindsay are having sex at college, but they're not comfortable with the young people sharing a room in their house. How should the Vaughns proceed?*

- *Should they tell Chuck not to come?*
- *Should they insist on separate bedrooms?*
- *Should they swallow their discomfort and adjust to the realities of the 21st century?*

The Panel Weighs In:

A.J.: *Their house, their rules. The Vaughns should show the kids to their separate rooms, while realizing they can't control what happens after dark.*

Suzanne: *If they do that, their disapproval of how the kids live at college will be evident. Instead, they should wave toward the bedrooms and let the young people decide what they're going to do.*

Billy: *The Vaughns should discuss the sleeping arrangements with Chuck ahead of time. That way there will be no awkwardness when the young people arrive.*

Laila: *If the Vaughns take a hard stand against pre-marital sex in their home, they have to be prepared for Chuck to reply that he's not coming. I'm not saying the Vaughns shouldn't stick to their guns, but they have to be aware of the possible fallout.*

You Again?

For the first time since records have been kept, the most common domestic arrangement for young American adults aged 18-34 is living in their parents' home, and fewer than 32% are residing independently with a spouse or partner. This represents a major shift from 1960 when only 20% of this age group lived with their parents and 62% lived with a "romantic partner," as the Pew Research Center refers to wives, husbands, and significant others.

Living Situation, Americans 18–34

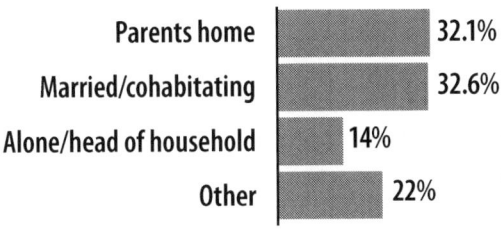

Parents home	32.1%
Married/cohabitating	32.6%
Alone/head of household	14%
Other	22%

"Alone/head of household" includes single parents and people who have roommates or renters living with them; "other" includes those living with family members (not parents), with nonfamily members, or in group housing.

Pew Research Center/NPR

Today, who is back at home or never left? More single young men live with their parents than do single young women; the less educated are also more likely to be found there than are their college-educated counterparts; and young adult blacks and Hispanics have been part of this movement since 1980. But the overall trend is the same for every demographic group—living with parents is increasingly common. Moreover, it's a worldwide trend: the number of young adults living with their parents is now 49% in Japan, 48% in the European Union, 42% in Canada, and 29% in Australia. All these figures are up from 20 years ago.

The reasons why

The conventional wisdom is that everything changed with the Great Recession, which began in 2007, and wage earners have struggled since then to regain the ground they lost. However, the rise in the number of young adults living at home started before the economic crash — and so did the possible contributing factors. Male unemployment has been on the rise for decades, according to the Pew Research Center, and those who have jobs having been making less than they would have in their parents' day adjusted for inflation.

But the main reason for the shift cited by Pew is that fewer young people are getting married. Even accounting for the increased popularity of cohabitation, they say there are just fewer paired-up 20-somethings and 30-somethings than there used to be. The median age at marriage has been rising for decades and a growing share of the Millennials are eschewing marriage altogether. Pew projects that fully one in four of today's young adults 18-34 may never get married, which does not bode well for those parents who long to one day be grandparents.

Crushing College Expenses

Ricki and Ted's daughter, Melissa, wants to go to a private, residential college halfway across the country, but her parents want her to take the first two years at the local community college, which is a much better fit for their budget. Melissa has dug in her heels, countering that they went to private colleges, so why shouldn't she have the same opportunity? When they point out that higher education cost a pittance then compared to what it costs now—and even so they're still paying off their student loans—Melissa retorts, "Fine, if it's such a hardship for you, I'll just get a job and skip college altogether." What should Ricki and Ted do?

- Stick to their guns and insist she start out at home?
- Take her dare and let her get a job instead of going to college?
- Capitulate and tap into their retirement funds?

The Panel Weighs In:

Dan: *Melissa should stay home, work, and go to community college at night and on weekends, while saving up for her junior and senior years at the private college. It will be invaluable for her to see how hard it is to make money and how easy it is to spend it.*

Georgia: *Even though she sounds like a brat, Melissa's desire to go away to school is totally understandable. I'd help her fulfill her dream, but I'd insist that she make out a budget—which includes her getting a part-time job—to show how it could work financially.*

Johanna: *It's horrible to have to choose between your child's education and your retirement, but that's a reality of life today. I'd hope Ricki and Ted would insist that Melissa start out at home. The private college will still be there in two years.*

Bennett: *I'd take Melissa up on her dare. Let her see how hard it is to get a job as a mere high school graduate and how boring the work is that would be open to her. After this experience, she'll value both her parents and higher education all the more.*

When It's Time for Them to Move Out

Often when a child returned home from college or the military or never got around to leaving in the first place, you and he thought of it as a short, interim situation. But over time it has started to look more and more like a long, permanent one. Between the "gig economy," student loans and the high price of real estate, it's not surprising that we've spawned a "boomerang" generation. Indeed, as I noted in "You Again?" more young adults are now living at home than at any time in the past 130 years. Sometimes it's great, but often it's not. After a while problems arise if your grown offspring has become oh-so comfy back in the nest, but you've grown weary of having a permanent boarder and there's no set time for him to exit.

Allison Bottke, author of *Setting Boundaries with your Adult Children* has a solution. Although Bottke's book basically deals with her struggles to parent her troubled adult son, her tough-love approach can be easily adapted by parents who, with the best of intentions, have become enablers, unwittingly hampering their child from living a fully functioning, independent life. To redress the situation she recommends forming a united front with your spouse if you have one. She further advises parents to make out a written action plan, sit down with their adult child to present it to him, and, finally, have him sign it, so there will be no ambiguity as to what's been agreed upon.

Here are some of Bottke's Do's and Don't's when it's time for your child to launch:

DO

- Set a firm move-out date.

- Be clear about what he can take with him in the way of furniture and supplies.

- Provide a transition care package. It might include the first month's rent and security deposit. State if it's a loan or a gift, your choice.

- Give him his health records and a list of medical providers.

- Gift him food coupons or grocery store gift certificates.

- Include a wall calendar.

- Assemble a small file box containing copies of such important papers as his birth certificate, DMV forms, and social security card.

DO NOT

- Negotiate.

- Give him money.

- Find him a place to live.

- Pack for him.

- Co-sign a lease or mortgage.

- Allow him to return home if things don't work out.

You can decide how hard nosed you want to be, and you may even find your child is secretly glad to finally have to leave. But if he's resistant, remember Lady Macbeth's rallying cry: "Screw your courage to the sticking place, and we'll not fail!"

When Speaking Up Is Risky

Charlene feels her daughter, Cara, is making the biggest mistake of her life by marrying her fiancé, Tim. In Charlene's opinion, Tim isn't Cara's equal in intellect, education, or earning power. Moreover, she doesn't like the way Tim orders her daughter around—is he a potential wife beater? Charlene's husband, on the other hand, thinks Tim is a good guy. He doesn't want his wife to voice her reservations, lest their daughter feel her parents don't have confidence in her ability to make good choices. What's a mother to do?

- Keep mum and let Cara make her own mistakes?
- Voice her reservations?
- Try to get Cara and Tim into prenuptial counseling?

The Panel Weighs In:

Liam: Charlene should have said something before Cara became engaged to Tim, but better late than never. She should find a diplomatic way to ask her daughter if she thinks Tim is a long-term proposition.

Juan: Charlene should practice watchful waiting. If a really big red flag surfaces, such as bruises on her daughter's body, she must speak up for safety's sake.

Mollie: Charlene has to zip it. Maybe Cara likes to be ordered around and maybe she sees qualities in Tim her mother doesn't. The dynamics of other people's relationships, even one's daughter's, are unknowable.

Kendra: I can see both sides of this situation. Besides, aren't poor choices what "starter marriages" are for?

Globalization Hits Home

After writing several pieces about the daughter-in-law from hell, I was pleasantly surprised to find the DIL from heaven. Either an immigrant or the child of immigrants, this family-minded individual really goes out of her way to please her husband's parents. Of course, there are differences to be overcome and adjustments to be made, but on the whole the parents I interviewed seemed very happy with their son's choice of a wife from another culture. Here's what they told me:

We all have preconceived notions

According to Greg J. "I am not proud of myself for this, but when my son said he was marrying a girl from Jordan, I blurted out, "Is she a Muslim?" We had a good laugh about this afterward because it turns out that *her* father's first words after hearing that his daughter was marrying an American were, "Is he a Muslim?" (And neither family is Muslim, by the way.)

"I thought all Asian women were submissive to their husbands," said Carrie P., "but our Chinese daughter-in-law often stands up to our son. In other ways, though, she is a product of her heritage in that she's more more respectful of her in-laws than an American-born girl would be, and we love her for that."

Said Sami G, "My older son married a girl from the Midwest, one of nine children whose parents are very committed Catholics. Since we're so East Coast in outlook and not in the least religious, I find her harder to relate to than my daughter-in-law from South Africa!"

The world is coming to you; get ready

The way people are taught to communicate varies from culture to culture, so even if your DIL speaks English really well, her presentation may be baffling. "My daughter-in-law from Hungary is beyond blunt," said Emma T. "She will say things like 'I'd never live in your house because it's too small and dark.' After two years of this, I've learned to depersonalize and, in some cases, be more blunt myself. To be fair, in this country women are brought up to be gracious and observe the social niceties. Perhaps she was brought up to survive."

And it's not only in the realm of communications but in customs that awareness needs to be raised. Said Fiona R., "I had to be coached in the etiquette of bringing gifts when we visit our Japanese daughter-in-law's parents. Designer labels seem to mean a lot to them, I found." Then there's the issue of inclusiveness. Nick Z. recounted, "We recently asked our son and his wife out to dinner, and before you know it we had her sister and brother-in-law, parents, aunts and uncles, too. It got to be quite a crowd, but I guess that's how they roll in Korea. "

Family get-togethers are so often built around food that it's no wonder the topic came up over and over again in my interviews. Nick Z. continued, "Is Korean ever an eating culture! It's a good thing we like their food because with them it's all kimchi all the time." Then Georgia S. told me, "At special Persian holidays—and there seem to be a lot of them—my sweet daughter-in-law cooks all kinds of exotic foods. My husband and I are not really into spices, but we're touched that she makes an extra-special effort, so we grin and bear it. Our own daughter should be so loving."

Diane H. told a similar tale. "Cuban cuisine seems to come in only three varieties: hot, hotter, and mouth on fire. The grandmothers around the table always scold me for eating like a bird, but I've learned that for me it's *el mínimo* of arroz con frijoles or *el máximo* of Alka-Seltzer. At the end, though, I always praise my daughter-in-law's culinary efforts in my limited high school Spanish, which makes her smile. She really gets what it means to be a family member, so we hug and kiss like we mean it, which we do."

Study up!

There's lots you can do to make things go smoothly with your DIL and her family. According to Jacqueline Oliveira, M.A., who conducts intercultural training for businesses, "The best way to bridge the cultural divide is to learn as much as you can about your daughter-in-law's heritage. Read books, ask questions, attend her place of worship, take part in her rituals, and ask her to teach you how to cook her traditional foods. What a great opportunity this is to expand your horizons while cementing your relationship with one of the most important people in your life."

So let's raise a toast to these dear daughters-in-law from abroad. Salud! Kanpei! Geonbae! L'chaim! Slainte! Cheers!

Wedding Blues

Dale and John Schmidt are committed Christians, who brought up their three children to say grace before every meal and attend church every Sunday. Now their middle son, Seth, is marrying a non-believer who chose a coworker—a man who got his officiant's license on the Internet the previous week—to conduct their wedding ceremony. How should the Schmidts handle it?

- Should they grin and bear it?
- Should they pressure Seth and his fiancée to use their minister?
- Should they boycott the wedding in protest?
- Should they encourage their future daughter-in-law to go to church with them?

The Panel Weighs In:

Joel: The Schmidts should discuss their feelings with their son, otherwise resentments will fester. However, no matter what the outcome of the discussion they have to attend the wedding to show support.

Missy: I think the Schmidts should keep their mouths shut and their ears open. Pressure can only backfire. It's the kids' day and all the choices about the wedding should be theirs alone.

Eduardo: The Schmidts should move beyond the wedding and build new family-oriented, religion-centered occasions that are meaningful to them.

Sujin: If Seth were such a devout Christian he wouldn't

agree to his fiancée's choice of officiant. Maybe his values are not as aligned with his folks' as they think.

Readers' Comments

They could ask their son how he feels about it and honor whatever he says—it might get him thinking. They will, OF COURSE, go to the wedding and comment no more! P.D.

Either go along or you'll find out that the elopement was great. L.K.

What Do You Owe Your Parents?

The Younger Generation Weighs In

Earlier this year I asked a number of parents about their feelings of obligation to their grown offspring. Their responses, which appeared in "What Do You Owe Your Adult Child?" ranged from "24/7 support" to "zilch." To balance out the picture, I recently created a questionnaire that Professor Susan Lang distributed to 25 undergraduates in two Psychology and Education seminars at Antioch University Santa Barbara. Their responses are far from statistically valid. Antioch students skew older than traditional undergraduates, most are on financial aid, and many come from ethnic families, which tend to be closer than non-ethnic families. Still, their responses give us a tantalizing peek into the younger generation's attitudes, which are as varied as those of the POGOs I interviewed before on this topic. Here are some representative quotes:

These grown children stay in touch

Most of the students reported speaking or texting and even visiting with their parents frequently, and in many cases are the ones initiating the contact.

> *"I feel obligated to have regular contact with my mother and check in with her first about holiday plans."*

> *"We speak three-four times a week. I have to make most of the calls because they think I'm so busy (which I am) that they don't want to 'bother' me."*

> *"My mother lives in town, so I have an obligation to*

touch base with her every day and on holidays."

"I feel I should keep them up to date on my life."

"I check in on their well-being regularly. I also listen to their complaints about each other!"

As they see their duty

Most of the students want to be there for their parents, but they like thinking it is voluntary as opposed to obligatory.

"I owe my parents my life, and I would be willing to give them anything I can."

"I owe them time to get to know them better and mend any wounds in our relationship."

"Handle my responsibilities and take care of myself."

"I don't want to be a burden to them, but they still give me money."

"The only thing I 'owe' them is to be happy. I would likely go out of my way for them if they needed me, but I don't feel like it's an obligation."

"I'd put my whole life on hold if they needed me."

"I do feel appreciative for everything they have done for me throughout my life and I want to do the same thing for them."

They are aware of their parents' expectations

Most of the students feel their parents want them to have families and successful careers. They hope to meet those expectations—sort of—but they don't feel it is their job in life to make their parents happy.

"My parents expect me to graduate from college and get a good job. I feel obligated to do this, but for me not them."

"I have those expectations for myself, too."

"My parents haven't set any expectations for me. They said they just want me to be happy."

"They have their own pursuits and my mom is happy with my stepfather and her friends. She is very happy that I have a child, though!"

"I want to show them I can do it."

"I want to make them happy and proud and help them avoid stress."

"I used to think it was my job to make my parents happy. Now I couldn't care less."

They feel they owe their parents a lot . . .

Not all but most of the students feel a great sense of obligation to their folks. Some of the words that came up repeatedly in their answers were respect, appreciation, love, communications, time, courtesy, patience, and acceptance, and present and available.

"I help out at home with my younger siblings. I make sure to celebrate with my parents and give them time off for their own dates."

"Give money, buy them stuff."

"No obligations, just genuine caring."

"Relieve their stress."

"I repay them by showing them honor and by being the man they raised me to be."

. . .And could be doing more

Sixteen students said, yes, they could be doing more and nine said no.

Yes

> *"I could do more but don't have the time. Some guilt associated with that."*
>
> *"I feel a little guilty because I'm not able to help my mother and father financially as much as I would like."*
>
> *"As they get older I feel I should help more around the house."*

No

> *"I already do too much."*
>
> *"I probably could be doing more , but I don't feel guilty about it. My parents weren't there for me much when I was little."*

They will care for their parents in the end

Three-quarters of the respondents expected to care for their parents, the other quarter didn't. Answers on both sides were:

> *"Never in my home, but I'm sure I'll end up paying for their care."*
>
> *"I expect to take care of my grandparents, who raised me, but not so much my parents."*
>
> *"Most likely I would relocate to care for them at their home."*
>
> *"My parents have been there for me and I would love to be there for them."*
>
> *"My obligation is to take care of them when they can't take care of themselves."*

Your children may never have thought about what they owe you. Are you brave enough to ask them?

Chapter 5

The Fractured Family

"Happy families are all alike; every unhappy
family is unhappy in its own way."
Leo Tolstoy

This oft-quoted first line from Anna Karenina is a fitting way to introduce issues in the fractured family. Some families never heal when the parents divorce, while some come through it with no noticeable scars. After the split many families recombine into new, "blended" families (the term that's now favored over "step-families"), but these new entities, too, often bring with them their own set of complications. Although the divorce rate for the younger generation is going down because fewer of them are getting married, it is on the rise among the older generation, often after long-term marriages.

When young people do get married, some of their unions are of the short-lived "starter marriage" variety. Some social critics decry this phenomenon as a sign that our society is crumbling. Others feel it makes more sense to divorce than hang onto a bad marriage "'til death do us part."

Of course, divorce, yours or your adult children's, isn't the only reason for discord. We now know that sibling rivalry can continue into adulthood, poisoning relations among both the nuclear and extended family. Finally, there are times when much to their chagrin, parents are drawn into their grown children's adulterous situations.

Divorce After a Long-Term Marriage

Although almost 50 percent of all marriages in the United States dissolve, that percentage has actually been declining slightly. At the same time the percentage of splits in longer-term marriages has been increasing. Researchers at Bowling Green State University found that the divorce rate among adults 50 and older more than doubled between 1990 and 2008, and those married more than 15 years now account for 20% of all divorces in the country.

Reasons vary

A number of reasons are cited for this new wave of "Silver Splitters," everything from people living longer, individuals wanting more out of life, greater economic freedom, empty nest syndrome, early retirement, less social stigma, and that old stand-by, adultery. But no matter what the cause, adult children often find themselves shocked and grieving when their parents' long-term marriage falls apart. Unfortunately, they have few places to go with their emotions. Unlike younger children of divorce, for whom concern and support are widespread, grown offspring are usually just expected to "deal with it." These adult children of divorce or ACOD's, as they are increasingly called, are finding their voice, and they have a lot to say about their parents' uncoupling.

Many decry the loss of boundaries. As one 33-year-old said, "I had my dad crying on one shoulder and my mom on the other." Others start to question all their assumptions about marriage. As a 28-year-old said, "All that togetherness that I've taken for granted for nearly three decades has disappeared. It's very upsetting." And still others wish their parents would not confide in them. They view their parents' stories of their sex life, infidelities, and marital disputes as Too Much Information.

Not only does "Gray Divorce" often have long-term, negative ramifications for the adult children's personal lives (including the greater likelihood of their own divorce), it can also sour their relationship with one or both of their parents, sometime for all time. A case in point is that of Sarah P. Sarah was married at the age of 19 and stay married for 35 years even though she had stopped loving her husband long before. Although she had a successful career, she nevertheless feared being a woman on her own and wanted to see her two daughters established before she left. A series of disastrous investments on her husband's part left them broke, which gave her the courage to finally call it quits.

Choosing up sides

After the divorce announcement, Sarah's daughters immediately took sides, and the side they chose was their father's. They were joined in battle by his extended family. "So," as Sarah puts it, "in one stroke I lost not only my husband, but my children and whole family." As is so often the case, the one who leaves is portrayed as the bad guy, and Sarah went from being a garden-variety mom to the devil incarnate. She wanted desperately for the whole family to go into therapy to repair the relationship, but the girls flatly refused and her husband only went twice, so she set to work by herself to repair the psychic fallout, and she worked hard at it. As part of one workshop, for example, she wrote a letter to the girls explaining the divorce from her point of view and asking for their understanding. The second step was calling them to right any perceived wrongs. Both daughters told her, "Never contact me again."

Many years after her divorce, Sarah has found love, enjoys a good relationship with the grandchildren, and leads a busy, productive life. She is convinced that she did the right thing in divorcing her husband (although she wishes she had done it sooner), and she knows she has to let go of the residual guilt and self-recrimination. Yet there's still a pocket of sadness in her heart that she can't seem to get rid of. "I care about people and these people didn't allow me to care about or for them," she says of her daughters. "That's my biggest loss."

Everything's More Complicated In Blended Families

Milo's 55th birthday is coming up and he wants to have a family gathering to celebrate. His grown children have made it clear they won't attend unless their mother is included, too. His new wife will not hear of it because of the bitter fallout from the split. How do you think he should handle it?

- *Give in to his kids?*
- *Give in to his new wife?*
- *Forget the party and take his wife on a cruise?*
- *Insist that everyone call a truce.*

The Panel Weighs In:

Jon: Milo's bitter first wife has no place at his milestone birthday. When there's a lot of residual anger, there's no way to pretend this is one big, happy family for a night. His second wife is right—and, besides, he has to continue living with her.

Janice: Under no circumstances should Milo give in to his kids, who are using the occasion to bully him. If he gives in to them now, there'll feel empowered to hold a whip over his head forever.

Debbie: Milo has to get a grip—on his family, that is. Everyone is trying to manipulate him, and they're losing sight of who's important here.

Riley: The cruise is looking better and better . . .

Wicked Stepmother of Myth

Better a serpent than a stepmother!
Euripides 438 B.C.

In every culture and every era stories have abounded about the evil woman who abused—and sometimes even murdered—her husband's children by his first wife. The yoke of this legacy hangs heavy around the neck of second wives, often lasting well into the time their stepchildren reach their majority. Let's look at four of iconic myths featuring the baddies of legend.

Snow White: The quintessential Wicked Stepmother is the queen in Snow White. She is so jealous of her stepdaughter's beauty that she orders the huntsman to take the young woman out into the forest, kill her, and bring back her heart and liver as proof that she's dead.

Cinderella: Then there's the cruel stepmother in Cinderella, who treats the girl as a servant and makes her life a living hell.

Hansel and Gretel: Thirdly, there's the me-first step-mother of Hansel & Gretel, who, when famine sweeps the land, convinces her husband to abandon the children from his first marriage so she and he will have enough to eat. (Of course, the fact that he went along with the scheme doesn't speak too well of him, either.)

Phaedra: Finally, there's the legend of Phaedra, the second wife of a Greek leader. She attempts to seduce her stepson, Hippolytus, but he rejects her. Outraged, she takes her revenge by saying Hippolytus raped her, an accusation that leads to his death.

A prominent characteristic of all these evil second wives of myth is jealousy of their stepdaughter's youth and beauty—"Mirror, mirror on the wall" anybody? Sometimes they display lust for their handsome stepson, and often they act out of greed to ensure that their husband's inheritance will go to their own biological children instead of his. In every instance they go to great lengths to achieve their ends.

The myth lives on

Unfortunately, the stereotype of the Wicked Stepmother doesn't show signs of vanishing anytime soon. Recently Amazon TV presented the series, Evil Stepmothers. Wherever they went, these arch-villains left murder, mayhem, and destruction in their wake. The first episode's title, "Not my Mom," may sum up the reason why the Wicked Stepmother myth is so persistent. According to Bruno Bettelheim and other psychologists, there's a common desire among children to offload the characteristics they don't like in their biological mothers onto an imaginary Bad Stepmother figure. Then they can hold onto another fantasy, that of the Perfect Real Mother.

Step-families have been a common occurrence throughout the ages, especially households in which the mother died in childbirth and the husband remarried. Today, step-families are much more likely to result from divorce, which has its own challenges and, occasionally, triumphs.

Liar, Liar, Pants On Fire

*C*issy, *Ian's young adult daughter, will stop at nothing to break up her father and his significant other, Julie. Trying to make nice, Julie took Cissy on a shopping trip to a nearby upscale mall and treated her to lunch. No sooner did Julie drop her off at home than Cissy was on the phone to her dad, filling his ear with made-up stories about how Julie spends money like a drunken sailor. Ian better not marry her, Cissy warned, or she'll quickly take him to the poorhouse. Knowing how frugal Julie is, Ian laughed it off and even teased her later about her alleged spending spree. Julie was furious. What should she do with her anger?*

- *Swallow it and pretend she doesn't know what Cissy is doing?*

- *Set Ian straight?*

- *Confront Cissy and tell her to stop trying to sabotage their relationship?*

The Panel Weighs In:

Steve: *The good news is that Ian is on to Cissy and laughed off her tell-all about the shopping trip. Going forward Julie should aim for simple civility—neither overtly friendly nor overtly nasty—and one day maybe Cissy will come around.*

Josie: *Julie has a right to feel hurt and angry, but she should talk to a counselor about her feelings rather than jeopardize her relationship with Ian. Venting her anger in front of either father or daughter will come to no good.*

Doug: *Julie should make sure Ian will stand up for her, and then she should bring up the incident with the three of them in the same room. When Cissy sees that she's been called out in front of her father, she'll think twice before pulling this kind of stunt again.*

Lois: *Julie should make a stand now with both Cissy and Ian. If they are to have a future, he's got to insist that Cissy treat Julie with the respect accorded a wife. If Ian refuses to take her seriously or reprimand his daughter, it's better that Julie find out now before she invests any more of herself in this relationship.*

A Child's Divorce, Part 1: How Parents Felt

When an adult child's marriage breaks up, his/her parents are often drawn into the fray. They are called upon to provide emotional, financial and sometimes, as with increased babysitting, even physical support. I spoke with several parents who have gone through it to see how they felt, how they fared, and how they would advise others in their situation to cope. With the divorce rate stubbornly hovering at around 50 percent, there's an even chance that you will be able to relate.

Wondered why. Maggie V. told me, "Both my sons made inappropriate marriages. How is it that my husband and I have been together contentedly for over fifty years and they couldn't make a go of it for even ten? Did they just assume a marriage would take care of itself? Or, since all of their friends' parents were divorced, maybe they thought that's the norm and we're the weird ones. Who knows? People who are constantly sniping at each other stay together while others who seem so in love split up. The longer I live the less I understand people, especially my own children."

Did not feel guilty. I found surprisingly little self-flagellation among my respondents, even those who had been divorced themselves or whose child had been divorced more than once. A few said their child was too immature when he got married or went into it for the wrong reasons. Many more, though, thought either their kids' marriage had been a bad fit from the get-go or it was the fault of the other spouse (who was usually described as "mentally unstable," "troubled," "dealing with many personal issues," or, as one father put it rather more bluntly, "wacko." While their child's divorce led to some self-examination, by and large the parents didn't feel they had played a role in the break-up.

Rejected "failure" . . . The parents I spoke with did not feel their child's divorce was a referendum on their own parenting or on their child's moral fiber. "Divorce is the failure of an institution not individuals," said Janey D. "My son was unrealistic, and the expectations failed. That's the extent of it," said Don P. Phil B. chimed in, "People make mistakes, childish mistakes, even when they're chronologically not children anymore. Others are simply not suited for marriage or can't seem to pick the right one." I've also heard some therapists voice concerns that the younger generation simply doesn't have what it takes to make a long-term relationship work.

. . . But experienced pain. "I felt awful for such a long time," Ellen R. told me. "I was miserable for my grandchildren, who were so upset, and I was frustrated that there was nothing I could do to make the situation right. In order not to step on their mother's toes, I always went through her to speak with the kids. When they were older I was able to have direct conversations with them, and they thanked me for being there for them. I guess we all weathered the storm, even if we'll never be exactly the same again."

Quelled impatience. DeeDee R. said, "My daughter knew it was over for at least ten years before she finally called it quits on her marriage. I think it was a combination of her perfectionism, loyalty, and desire to provide a stable home for her children that kept her from pulling the trigger. So, year-in, year-out I had to listen to her tales of woe while I zipped my lip. It was torture! When she finally made her move, it was all I could do from turning cartwheels, but I couldn't let my exuberance show because I knew she was still wracked by conflicting emotions. A year has passed and we have a much more relaxed, natural relationship now without my having to watch every word."

Breathed a sigh of relief. "It's much worse for children to live in a house where the parents are at war than one headed by a mother or father alone," contends Cindy A. "The constant conflict exacts a terrible toll on kids, who feel it's their fault and/or their place to make peace. No kid should have to go through that. Since the acrimony continues in my son's situation, both his children are still struggling emotionally even though by now they're both in college. I wish the split had come earlier for the kids' sake." But some splits have a happy ending. Bente J. told me, "My daughter-in-law called at the time of the divorce to say I would always have access to the grandchildren. God bless her! I slept for the first time in months after getting that phone call."

A Child's Divorce, Part 2: What Parents Did

*"Divorce makes it tempting for everyone
concerned to divide the world into good and
evil, victim and aggressor, villain and martyr.
Grandparents, aunts, uncles, cousins, and others
may all line up in hostile allegiance beside their
family member."*
Joshua Coleman, Ph.D. *When Parents Hurt*

In the last article, I looked at what parents *felt* as their child's marriage came apart. In this piece I'll examine what parents *did*.

Some swung into action . . . Jim D. said, "I was in the trenches with my daughter. She was all shook up over the split, so I took charge. I was the one who found her a locksmith, a family lawyer, and a good therapist. When her ex sued to get full custody of the children—and failed—I made sure he repaid the court costs to *me* to remind him every month not to pull a stunt like that again. He can push around my daughter, but he knows he can't do that to me."

Johanna G. said, "I just couldn't sit on the sidelines while my grandchildren suffered so during this time of terrible upheaval. I stepped up financially so that the kids and my daughter-in-law could stay in their home. My son stopped talking to me for a while over this, but I felt I simply had to stabilize the situation." Liz B. added, "I offered to pay for therapy for the kids. My son's ex took me up on it, and it proved to be a great way for them to pour out their hearts in a safe environment."

. . . Others purposely did nothing. "We tried to stay as far away from the divorce as possible, just as we had tried to stay away from the marriage. We felt we had no constructive role to play when things were good, and we certainly didn't have any role to play when things got bad. Toward the end our daughter-in-law would call and say, 'Come up right now and you deal with him!' Then she would send us vicious emails. We never responded. Unfortunately, her weapon of choice was the grandchildren, whom she kept from us for ten years. When we finally got to see them and tactfully inquired why their mother was so dead set against us, they replied, 'She said you were mean to her.'"

Most listened—ad nauseum. Said Bradley S., parent of a divorcing son. "The last person in the world your child wants to get advice from is his father. So, unless I'm asked for my opinion directly, I nod, say 'uhm', or spout something innocuous. I have to respect him as an adult even if he is not living according to my values. Besides, this is the world's worst time to be judgmental. He's such a mess that anything I say will be taken as criticism." According to Marsha Temlock, MA, author of *Your Child's Divorce: What to Expect—What You Can Do,* you should be supportive, ask how you can help, and validate your child's feelings, but don't pile on about the ex, as tempting as that may be. "You're going to see a certain amount of regression," she says, "Your child may feel very, very needy."

They pitched in with the grandchildren. The experts say making your home a refuge for the grandchildren is one of the most important things you can do. Their entering a conflict-free zone and repeating familiar rituals will be a great comfort to the kids, even if they don't articulate it. Rachel D. was appreciative that, "My divorced son's sister really spent a lot of time and energy ensuring that her nephews knew they were embedded in a strong, loving family." And Chris P. offered, "My own ex and I tried to set a good example by attending family events together to show the kids it was possible to be cordial after a divorce."

Many dug into their retirement funds. Adina M. said, "We sacrificed a big chunk of our savings account to help out our daughter when her ex stopped making his child support payments. She works as a teacher, but that doesn't cut it in Los Angeles. I know you're not supposed to make your kids too dependent on you, but the "experts" who dispense that advice clearly have not been in this situation themselves. Despite what you read about million-dollar celebrity settlements and big palimony payouts, divorce still leaves most women much poorer than when they were married."

They looked for the silver lining. "When my son-in-law moved out, the grandkids could start the healing process, so that was a plus," said Kelly M. Karen L. offered, "I think my daughter's divorce brought his sibs and me closer. We all worked on her relationship together." Aaron P. added, "Since the divorce my son confides in us more than in the past." Lisa Z. chimed in, "I've gotten past the worst of it, and I've come to realize that my ex-daughter-in-law has problems of her own." Pam K. had the final word: "After two failed marriages to damaged human beings, my son is finally tired of his Mr. Fix-It role. I'd like to see him try again if he wants to—but only with the right person."

What's Fair?

When Jim moved into a house with his son, Ethan, eight years ago, they agreed to split the rent 50–50. Since then Ethan has married and had two children—effectively leaving Jim with just one space to call his own, his bedroom—yet they're still splitting the rent 50–50. What should Jim do?

- *Have a heart-to-heart with Ethan about the unfairness of the current split?*

- *Find another roommate?*

- *Ignore his daughters and keep paying half?*

The Panel Weighs In:

Walt: *If Jim feels that he's paying the same or less than he would be in another living situation and loves being with his family, he shouldn't rock the boat by bringing up the subject of rent with his son.*

Gayle: *Ethan is no doubt snowed under with all the additional expenses of young children, but his family should at least vacate the living room at certain times so Jim can have some grownup time in his own home.*

Michelle: *Jim should let Ethan know he has to pay more since he has four people living in the house to Jim's one. Fair is fair.*

Jeremy: *Jim should move out. It's been too long, the circumstances have changed too drastically, and it's now too awkward to bring up the rent split. Time for Jim to go.*

A Mother's Regret: When Grown Siblings Don't Get Along

by Terry Haward

Years ago, when I found out I was pregnant with my second child, I knew what I wanted fervently in my heart. There was none of this "Oh, I don't care if I have a boy or a girl—I just want the baby to be healthy" stuff. I wanted a girl. More specifically, I wanted my older daughter, then age 4, to have a sister.

I got my second girl, and my daughter got a sister—and now it's 20 years later, and they don't like each other at all.

My own sister-the-role-model

When I was in sixth grade, my sister was a senior in high school. I used to carry her yearbook picture in my wallet—she was so glamorous, so pretty, so grown-up. I'd show it off to my friends. Six years apart, we never fought growing up, because she was almost in another generation, always ten steps ahead. I followed like a puppy behind her.

When she was 10 she started piano lessons, and I—age 4—insisted on them, too. She majored in journalism in college and got a job as a reporter; I worked my way through college in part via a writing gig and got a job in publishing right after graduating. (She switched careers after a few years; I, decades later, am still working with words.) For a couple of years, our jobs were in the same office building in New York City. Imagine the chances of that, all those buildings in the vast city, and we worked five floors apart, one of us at a law firm, the other at a publishing house.

She moved to Brooklyn; I moved to Brooklyn, five blocks away. She moved to Queens; I moved to Queens. She moved to Jersey; I moved to Jersey, two towns away. Then we both moved to the town in between us, and now we live a mile apart.

She is my Person, my favorite person. We talk almost daily and text multiple times a day. Our kids mistake us for each other. If we go to the same store at different times, we'll often walk out with the same shirt. No matter where I am or what I'm doing, I feel connected to her.

I wanted this for my daughters, but it hasn't worked out that way.

Two adorable small children

My favorite childhood photos of my daughters are the ones when they're cuddled under a blanket together. Lucy, a sassy 6 year-old, posing for the camera and flashing a V with her hand—I know she was saying "Girl Power!"—and 2-year-old Becca looking up at her with great concentration as she tried and failed to get her fingers to do the same. The two of them lying opposite head-to-feet in Lucy's bed, with Becca's toes nestled under Lucy's chin.

Photos like that break my heart. They weren't the best of pals—being four years apart put them in different lifetime zones—but they curled up together watching cartoons, drew pictures together, piled into our bed at night with their stacks of books. They had the normal sister arguments, all with the undercurrent of "That's not fair!" and the calculations of who was getting more and who was losing out.

My older daughter demanded more of the attention and got it. She was always highly verbal and talked over and through everyone else. She had some phobias and anxiety growing up that we needed to focus on; plus, she was the first so every parenting challenge seemed fraught. I worked full time, with an hour commute each way, and struggled to have enough time for each of them. Sometimes, the quieter child misses out.

Still, there was no unusual tension as they grew up. When Becca hit a stage that Lucy had already passed through (like the emo, black-eye-liner-tragic-music phase), Lucy had no patience for it, in that tendency we all have for disparaging what we've survived. She was quick with the biting comment; Becca was quick with the well-timed kick. When they each went through periods of depression and anxiety after their father died, it occasionally bonded them together but more often pushed them apart.

The split

A year ago, at ages 20 and 24—both of them living at home—they had a terrible, awful fight with long-ranging consequences. Lucy, the wronged party in this battle, moved in with my sister for a while. I would stop in and see her in the morning before work, and she'd come by to see the pets when Becca wasn't home. They each trash-talked the other to me; they each accused me of favoring the other. Caught in the middle, I could only keep repeating: *You're sisters, and at some point, you'll want and need each other. Weeks passed, then a month, and beyond.*

My mother-in-law wasn't close to her sister, her only sibling, as they were growing up. She didn't talk about her (and honestly, I didn't like her much, so I didn't ask), except for one story she told me soon after her son and I were married: When her mother had died 20-plus years before, her sister had made off with the linens, the lace tablecloths, and the damask napkins. "We never spoke again," she told me. "I was so angry!" She clearly still was.

Would this big chill between Lucy and Becca turn into a frozen tundra, I wondered, be too big to easily cross? I asked her if, over the years, she'd ever been tempted to reach out to her. "Nope," she said. "She stole the linens, my mother's linens, right out from under me!" She pursed her lips and shook her head. It seemed so petty. Imagine not speaking to someone again because of an argument over fabric. They're both dead now, never having reconciled. My husband and his sisters never had an aunt, didn't get to hear her stories about their mom as a kid.

I couldn't and still can't imagine anything that my sister could do or steal or say that would make me stop talking to her. Would this big chill between Lucy and Becca turn into a frozen tundra, I wondered, too big to easily cross?

Starting to reconcile

About six weeks into the freeze, I got a text from each of my daughters, a minute apart. *I saw Becca at the Toucan/I saw Lucy at the Toucan.* The Toucan was the only hip coffee place in town, and it was kind of amazing that they hadn't run into each other before. I called Lucy first. "It was okay," she said. "We nodded at each other."

A week later, they ran into each other there again and spoke a few words. A few weeks after that, Lucy moved back in, mainly because she missed the pets, she said. In the months since, there have been flare-ups but no horrendous fights, and they try to stay out of each other's way. The other day, I was sitting on the couch next to Becca, consoling her as she cried over a guy, and Lucy came in and hugged her.

They're not ready to hear this yet—there's still so much anger under the surface—but at some point, I'll tell them each this: *There will come a time when your sister will be the only one who also remembers your childhood. She'll be the only one who also remembers how Dad's taco casserole tasted and the look on my face when I showed up carrying our new puppy. She'll be the only one who knew about Dad's vast dorky tie collection, and how I unconsciously push my rice into a neat pile and pat it with my fork before eating it. Or about our early morning walks at our rented beach house, saving the horseshoe crabs and putting them back in the water. About the awful trip to Colonial Williamsburg in the 105 degree heat, with the murky warm pool at the sketchy hotel.*

At some point, you'll need, and want, to be each other's back-up memory banks—because our memories and our stories are so much of who we are, and who we eventually become.

This article by Terry Haward first appeared in the website, www.NextTribe.com.

Sibling Rivalry to the Max

M ark and Vicky Hadley's adult son and daughter can't stand each other. They didn't get along as youngsters, and the crack between them has widened to a chasm over the years. It makes family get-togethers impossible and prevents the grandchildren from bonding with their cousins. Should the Hadleys:

- *Bow to reality and visit with the two families separately?*

- *Insist that everyone suck it up on big occasions?*

- *Offer to fund a mediator to get the situation resolved?*

The Panel Weighs In:

Regina: I go with number one: Mark and Vicky should see the families separately so they can enjoy them tension-free.

John: No, absolutely not! A couple of times a year those kids can declare a truce in deference to their parents' wishes.

Andy: I like the mediator idea. I believe people have the capacity to change, and the rewards of a better adult family life are worth the gamble.

Julie: I don't know where I stand on all this except for the siblings' complaining about each other. The parents should not only not listen to the complaints. It only upsets them and lends credence to the kids' petty peeves.

Solution-Focused Therapy

Estrangement is a painful fact of life in many American families, and, based on anecdotal evidence, it seems to be increasing. Fortunately, ways have been developed to combat this sad situation, and one of the most promising is the short-term, guided approach known as solution-focused therapy or SFT.

Parent-child conflict

While often used with married couples on the brink of divorce, SFT has also been applied successfully to parent/adult child conflict. As its name implies, this approach is goal-oriented and collaborative, and it's structured to get results fast. In fact, resolution can often be reached in as few as three to ten sessions.

Stuart Light, a Licensed Marriage and Family Therapist in private practice, employs SFT. He kicks it off with what he calls "discernment counseling," a fact-finding session that establishes whether both sides are truly committed to making positive changes in their relationship. He does this by asking three questions:

- What brought you to this point?
- What have you done to try to repair your issues and solve your problems?
- What were the best times in your history together?

Then, using a technique common to mediation, he separates the parties. He talks to them individually for 20 minutes each about the path they would like to be on with each other. Afterward, they come back into the room together and honestly tell how they feel, what they want to work on, and what they want to change. They discuss what realistically can be changed. Together, they set goals.

Light says discernment counseling brings honest feelings to the surface. It establishes whether one side really has no interest in reconciliation, prefers the status quo—as disruptive and conflicted as it may be— or if everyone is committed to making things better. According to Light, "Both parties must have two feet in the circle. If that's the case, the odds of success with solution-based therapy are 70–80 percent. If that's not the case, it just isn't going to work."

The therapist's role is key

The role of the therapist is critical. According to Light, this third party is part referee and part witness, who is tasked with setting boundaries and enforcing strict guidelines. Name calling and interrupting are out; respectful listening is in. He says, "Family members are not adept at communicating with one another when things go wrong. They start blaming, shaming, pushing all the old buttons, and dredging up ancient history. A slugfest may be satisfying to the participants at the moment, but it's unproductive. With SFT we look at the past only insofar as it illuminates how we got where we are, but, basically, we focus on the present and future and how to make them better. Our only goal is to fix the relationship. SFT gives family members the tools to do so going forward."

Mediation Agreement

Another avenue for overcoming estrangement is working with a general mediator, which is the route taken by one of our readers—and it worked. She shared the document that emerged from her successful session:

Parent and adult child agree to accept each other as they are now. They don't have to like what the other does or how the other one is, but they agree to accept each other as they are. Parent and adult child agree to a new way of communicating with one another.

1. Coming from the "I" place: For instance, "When you say x, it makes me feel defensive and then I close off." The person responding to this does not have to respond immediately; they can ask for time to think things over, or they can answer in any appropriate way, understanding that they have simply received information.

2. They agree to talk about themselves without using comparisons, like "I feel x, but you don't."

3. They agree not to label one another i.e. "You are…"

4. They agree to check out assumptions with each other.

5. They agree to help each other stick to this model of communication.

6. They acknowledge each others' perceptions and feelings. For example, "I understand that you see it this way, and I can accept that as your view even though mine is different."

7. When talking about a third party, it is important to include him or her. For instance, "This is my perception of how x is feeling, but check it out with her."

8. Don't try to get a third person to support or accept or buy into your perception. Do not try to get an ally.

9. Use the style of no "wrong" or "right," but rather just different perceptions.

10. Talk of yourself not someone else, i.e. "My perception is x" rather than "Our perception is x."

11. The intention of the above is to open up communications, not close them off.

12. After three months, parent and adult child will assess the effect of the above on their relationship and decide together if they want to continue or modify anything.

If You See Something, Say Something?

Denise and Phillip's son, Scotty, was meeting a friend for drinks at a downtown bar when he was horrified to see his brother-in-law, Greg, wrapped around a woman—a woman who was not Jackie, his sister and Greg's wife. Scotty told his parents what he saw and now they're in a terrible quandary.

- Should they keep silent rather than break up Jackie's marriage?
- Do they owe it to Jackie to let her know what's going on?
- Should they seek guidance from a family and marriage counselor?

The Panel Weighs In:

Andy: You never know—Greg and Jackie may have an open marriage and this might be acceptable behavior to them. Even so, Denise and Phillip should hire a private investigator to find out if what Scotty saw is really an affair. If so, then they should go to a marriage counselor to learn the best way to break the news to Jackie. One way or the other, they have an obligation to tell their daughter.

Roger: The family owes it to Jackie to tell her, but they need a cooling-off period. They also need professional help in framing the discussion. This is a really sensitive issue!

Alyssa: Denise and Phillip should meet with Greg and give him 24 hours to explain it all to his wife. Otherwise, they're going to go to her with what Scotty saw. They don't need to know the details but Jackie does. Hopefully, it's a misunderstanding or something Greg and Jackie can work out. If they do stay together, the parents don't want to be caught in the middle.

Sandi: This is very tough, but ultimately it will be between the husband and wife. The parents should proceed cautiously because maybe Jackie doesn't want to know and/or she could figuratively shoot the messenger. It would be better if Jackie found out on her own, which she inevitably will, because if Greg is carrying on in a public bar, it's only a matter of time until his infidelity is discovered. Then Jackie is the one who has to decide: keep her husband, dump him, or find out if he's willing to work on their marriage.

Chapter 6

Staying In Touch With Your Feelings and Each Other

When things aren't going smoothly with you and your adult children or they are not setting the world on fire, it's the most natural thing in the world for you to question your earlier parenting. Second-guessing, weighing nature against nurture, and feeling guilty are recurring themes in my readers' comments, especially if they are the parents of young adults. Another trope is how hurt, angry, and disregarded they feel when their adult children fail to get back to them promptly or at all.

The following poem about a Mother's Day gone awry, *Flowers and Empathy* by Linda Schwartz, garnered many comments. Here's a particularly articulate one: "The power of these artificial holidays created by Hallmark looms large in the American consciousness, including mine. Decades of images by Norman Rockwell and others of perfect, all-American, multi-generational families glowing at holidays have really done a number on our heads. Even when we know intellectually this is a fantasy, we can't help feeling emotionally that somehow we should be achieving that level of blissful togetherness. Everyone wants to feel embedded in some way, and 'family' can be created in so many ways today."

Flowers and Empathy

by Linda Schwartz

they call to say they can't make it home
for Mother's Day this year
other plans   other obligations
I tell myself to let it go
    not be hurt   disappointed
    but the heart can't be fooled

    my husband takes me to my favorite restaurant
    for dinner   just the two of us
    we dine surrounded by a sea of tables
    mothers laughing   celebrating the day
    with sons   daughters   grandchildren

    on our deserted island
    he brings flowers and empathy
    to fill the emptiness
    as I sit wishing
    for this endless day
    to end

Linda Schwartz is the author of Reflections: Poems about Life, Relationships, and Family.

Advice: How to Give It and When to Zip It

No subject is more fraught when it comes to parent/ grown child relations than advice: the giving of it, the taking of it, the consequences of it. In every culture and age elders were respected for their wisdom. In fact, they were the leaders of the community as priests, generals, medicine men, judges, chiefs—you name it. In the United States they were the pillars of the community.

Disregarded and disrespected

Then, a funny thing happened on the way to the 21st century in America: the parental generation was suddenly disregarded and disrespected. On TV and in movies, fathers went from authority figures to ineffectual bumblers and mothers went from saints to meddlesome yentas. Hippies said, "Don't trust anyone over 30", psychiatrists said, "It's all the parents' fault," and kids said, "They don't even know how to turn on the computer." As I came to realize through the research for my book, *Children Through the Ages: A History of Childhood,* the age of self-conscious parenting was upon us. Ancestor worship was out; child worship was in, and we're seeing the results in our grown children.

A lot of parents are afraid to open their mouths lest their grown offspring jump down their throats. To stay on good terms with their children, they refrain from sharing all they've learned from their decades on this planet. That's a lot of accumulated wisdom down the drain. But, according to Elizabeth Wolfson, PhD, who teaches in the

Masters of Clinical Psychology Department at Antioch University Santa Barbara, there's a valid reason for the adult children's attitude.

"Young adults generally don't seek advice from their parents, in part, because they are developmentally at a place of separating from parents and cultivating their own adult identities," she says. "Parental advice may then be interpreted as criticism that they are somehow not doing it right or are not capable of establishing their own adulthood. And despite the "wisdom of experience" parents may be able to offer, most of us need to learn experientially, that is, by making our own mistakes."

The frustration level is high

All this leaves parents frustrated because they love their children and feel they can help them make better choices or at least save them from making disastrous ones. And, yes, they still want to feel they play an important part their children's lives. Moreover, if a parent feels she must continuously walk on eggshells to preserve it; if she must be the ever-enthusiastic cheerleader endorsing every move her adult child makes, even if that move is off the walls; if her role is just to be a walking, talking smiley face—how fulfilling is that?

In giving advice psychotherapist Elizabeth Wolfson, PhD, suggests, "First be aware of your own agenda and frustrations. Examine your motives and challenge your certainty that what you know to be best may not be best for your child. You are in a true dilemma of instinctively wanting to protect your child while not being able to. There is nothing bad or wrong with that—it is nature taking its course. But it may not be what your child wants or needs.

"Your challenge is to bite your tongue," Dr. Wolfson continues, "and follow your children's lead. Are they asking for your input? Are they sending double messages about seeking advice and then rejecting it? Cultivating an adult identity separate from one's family of origin is a confusing and tricky endeavor filled with mixed feelings.

Diplomacy is a must

When you feel you absolutely, positively must weigh in (or are asked for your opinion), I suggest you keep your tone as neutral as possible. It is a delicate dance potentially filled with missteps and stumbles. Provide advice and insights gently, communicating that these are just your thoughts and of course, you know your adult children will do it in the way that suits them. Couch your advice in terms of "it's been my observation," or "what's worked for me is," or "here's how I see it "—and then sit down and clam up.

"If you think your children are really in trouble, you can ask what their supports might be and whether they have considered professional support (counseling). Ultimately, it's THEIR life. They know themselves better than you do, and the world they are negotiating is different from the one in your frame of reference. The most powerful thing you can do is communicate your confidence in your adult children's judgment and ability to make good decisions. Then disengage and focus energy on your own life while staying loving and available should they need you."

Second-Guessing Your Parenting?

I recently sat down with biological psychiatrist, Paul Markovitz, MD, PhD, to discuss the age-old debate of nature vs. nurture. The conversation had barely gotten started when Dr. Markovitz declared unequivocally that what we do as parents has little impact on how our kids turn out! I found his message both liberating and depressing—and terribly disorienting. It seemed so counterintuitive, flying in the face of everything we were told about cause and effect in child rearing. Yet, according to Dr. Markovitz, scientific studies prove it is 89–96 percent in the genes. Yikes! Until now I had always sided with author Isaac Bashevis Singer who said, albeit tongue in cheek, "Of course, I believe in free will. What choice do I have?"

Here are the main takeaways from my conversation with Paul Markovitz:

It's all in the genes. According to Dr. Markovitz: "In the past those who insisted nurture was what counted in child rearing based their conclusions more on loose observations and associations than on rigorous research. In recent years we have had many excellent studies, particularly those done of twins, that show similarities of personality, behaviors, mental health or illness, intelligence, sense of humor, even tastes in food and movies, that are astounding, especially when the twins were reared in different households. These are not learned but inborn characteristics." Dr. Markovitz feels it's all explained beautifully in the best-seller, *The Gene: An Intimate History* by Siddhartha Mukherjee. I would add *The Nurture Assumption: Why Children Turn Out the Way They Do* by Judith Rich Harris, which also supports Dr. Markovitz's position.

Children are not your report card. Dr. Markovitz says, "I believe that most parents do the best they can. But should they mess up, even to the extreme of molestation and deprivation, children who are 'tuned normal' will still come out okay. If a kid turns violent, it's more likely that he had the genetic predisposition for violence than that he mimicked his parents' anti-social behavior. Childhood trauma has often been trotted out as the reason certain children went off the rails. In my experience and research, though, there is nothing you can do as parents that will change the outcome for aberrant behavior or mental illness. We find this hard to accept because we like rational arguments, and we want to feel that how we brought up our children made a difference. I would just urge parents to accept their children as they are and not as a reflection of the job they did years ago. We all have our limitations—and they are inborn."

It's not you, it's their genetic makeup. Dr. Markovitz says, "Parents are convenient whipping boys for people in therapy. I have seen patients who are well into their fifties and even sixties who are still blaming their parents but not working to better their lives. My wife says there are 'wallowers' and 'doers' in this world, and they clearly are 'wallowers.' When bad things happen to psychologically healthy people, we mourn or get mad, but we move on with our lives. The 'wallowers' are wired to blame. Conversely, there are those who inherited the genes for good problem solving and high intelligence, looking—the proud parents would say—a lot like them. When things go wrong with their offspring, parents can still blame themselves if they like, but it should be for passing along undesirable genes— which might very well go back to great-grandparents and skip a generation or two—but not for their childrearing practices."

Go forward realistically. Dr. Markovitz concludes, "When it comes to mental illnesses, it is now understood that these are inherited, physical conditions. The psychiatric field is moving toward a hybrid model with pschyopharmacology first and therapy second. Genetic testing is also a very hopeful development, and I believe we will eventually be able to tailor treatment to the specific hard wiring of each patient. But to return to the original question of nature versus nurture in child rearing, in the end it doesn't matter. If something is wrong, the physician still has to change it. And even when most things are right with our grown offspring, we have to accept the fact that they and we were dealt certain cards genetically. Our only option is to play them as best we can."

Reader's Comment

This is so reassuring, not only in terms of offspring, but also siblings who we had trouble relating to or living with. It seems so appropriate to blame ourselves, but now I see a lot of it was preordained. G.M.

Feeling Guilty

When I asked Elizabeth Wolfson, PhD, faculty in the Clinical Psychology Department at Antioch University Santa Barbara, what is parental guilt? she laughed, "Ask a Jewish mother and you'll know!" For most of us a moderate amount of guilt is actually a sign of love and of a strong attachment to our offspring, but when guilt gets out of hand, it is unproductive and self-defeating.

What do we feel guilty about? According to Ann Smith, Executive Director of Breakthrough at Caron, the top 20 reasons parents experience remorse are:

- I wasn't there enough.
- I didn't listen.
- I was too focused on the house and work.
- I wasn't affectionate enough.
- I was critical.
- I yelled, hit, and blamed.
- I was a bad role model.
- I didn't take the time to understand my children.
- I wasn't consistent.
- I pushed too hard.
- I didn't push enough.
- I spanked.
- I drank.
- I was depressed.
- I fought with my children's dad or mom.

- I got divorced.
- I said hurtful things.
- I was selfish.
- I ignored my child.
- I didn't protect my children.

"All conscientious parents want to create the optimal childhood for their offspring," says Dr. Wolfson, "but we find out very quickly we can't, because the world is imperfect and we don't get to protect our children from this. This realization is particularly hard for new parents who are high achievers. They never failed at anything, so how could they fail at this? especially when they're trying so hard to do it not just right but perfectly."

No such thing as a perfect childhood

Dr. Wolfson advises, "You don't have as much power as you think, which should come as a relief. There's the influence of society, the media, other kids, and, above all, genetics. Besides, looking back, how were you to know the ingredients that would make for a 'perfect' childhood? You could only do your best with who you were at the time and who your children were. The good news is that, since life is full of challenges, any adversity they experience helps them learn skills that contribute to self-reliance later on."

Of course, if your adult child is thriving, it's easier to pat yourself on the back. If he or she is experiencing difficulties in forming relationships, holding a job or beating opioid addiction, you're much more likely to experience self-blame. Dr. Wolfson encourages parents of adult children to take a step back and ask themselves, "Do I really have that much power?"

Few of us were the Mother Theresa of parenting, meeting every one of the professional advice givers' impossible standards. We were then and are now just people, imperfect, unpredictable, and inconsistent, Yet we are also resilient and capable of change. We can't rewrite history, but, according to Elizabeth Wolfson, we can effect change by using our parental guilt to do things differently. Instead of wallowing in *could-a, would-a, should-a* thinking, we could try, for example, to be less controlling, softer, and more supportive.

Finally, let's say you've done the work on yourself and you're free at last of the heaviest burdens of guilt. Does that make you a less caring or worse parent? The experts say a resounding No! So for heaven's sakes, don't engage in what I call "raiser's remorse." Feeling guilt about not feeling guilty would be the ultimate irony.

5 Signs of Manipulation

by Jeffrey Bernstein, PhD

As a psychologist working with children and teens for over 30 years, I have counseled many troubled, overly dependent adult children. It is heart-wrenching to see these young adults in a self-defeating holding pattern with little motivation, and financially draining. The young adults suffer from substance misuse, depression, anxiety, and very low self-esteem.

They can be master manipulators

Troubled adult children often are master manipulators of their frustrated, desperate-feeling parents. They know the guilt-triggering painful comments to say to their emotionally exhausted, vulnerable parents such as, "Okay, great if you are not going to help me then I will just end up on the street and die!" Or, "All you do is tell me to get a job, stop pressuring me or I will kill myself." Sadly, your guilt, which in most cases is not justified, makes you vulnerable to the manipulations of your troubled adult child.

Parents of struggling adult children often to go "all or nothing" in looking at their situation: Either the struggling adult child needs to be let sink or swim or the parents are okay nurturing the struggling adult along. The answers are not always so black or white.

Guilt muddies the waters for parents of troubled adult children. Guilt plays tricks on the mind. It can convince you that your child's struggles are your fault. But given the role of genetics, negative peer influences, and personality characteristics that come in to play, parents would do well to serve themselves up some healthy doses of self-compassion. As my best friend from kindergarten says, "The only perfect people are in the cemetery!" So, if you've done something about which you're ashamed, apologize to your adult child and move on. Do your best not to dwell on it, otherwise it can continually serve as a manipulation tool by your adult child.

Following are five red flags that your adult child is manipulating you:

1. Your adult child holds you emotionally hostage by threatening to hurt or kill herself or himself. Adult children who are truly at risk for self-harm need to be taken seriously. But repeated, guilt inducing, manipulative, toxic plays for attention or leniency to get out of facing responsibilities needs to be directly called out and addressed.

2. You hear lying through "selective memory." You swear you had a conversation about a plan and everyone was pumped up and on the same page, But then one day, your adult child pretends to remember the conversation completely differently, if at all.

3. Your adult child does not take life on—but you do. You are shouldering his or her debt, taking on a second job, or taking on additional responsibilities while your adult son or daughter is caught up in inertia, being seemingly endlessly non-productive. You and your spouse or other family members feel strain created by the excessive neediness from this overly dependent adult child.

4. Your adult child "borrows" money from you because she or he can't maintain solid or consistent

employment. He says he intends to pay you back but that never happens. Yes, it is okay to help adult children out financially at times, as long as you are not being exploited in doing so.

5. You're resigned to disrespect. You think that because your adult child has "problems" that lets him or her off the hook from showing heartfelt respect. You may notice that he or she seems respectful when wanting something from you. Your adult child, however, turns on a dime or gets passive-aggressive if you refuse the request. You feel worn down and accept this emotional chaos as normal.

Tips for breaking free from your adult child's manipulations:

- Be calm, firm, and non-controlling in your demeanor as you express these guiding expectations below to motivate your adult child toward healthy independence.

- Set limits on how much time you spend helping your child resolve crises. Encourage the child to problem-solve by asking, "What are your ideas?" Then politely say something like, "I believe in your resourcefulness and know you'll feel better about yourself when you give this some further thought."

- Set firm boundaries with your child if he's constantly using your guilt to manipulate you. My book, *10 Days to a Less Defiant Child*, applies to including older ones as well. It discusses the Calm, Firm, and Non-Controlling approach, which teaches parents how to set boundaries while avoiding fruitless and destructive power struggles.

- While living with you, encourage working children to contribute part of their pay for room and board. If unemployed, have them help out around the house with gardening, cleaning, or other chores.

- Don't indiscriminately give money. Providing spending money should be contingent on adult children's efforts toward independence.

- Develop a response that you can offer in the event that you are caught off guard. For example, the next time you get an urgent text that says, "I need money," respond by saying, "I'll have to talk it over with your father [or, if you are single, "I'll have to think it over"] and I'll get back to you tomorrow." This will allow you time to consider it and give you a chance to think and talk about it beforehand. It will also show that you are remaining steady in your course while presenting a united front.

- Remember that you always have the right to say "I changed my mind" about a previous promise.

- Remember you are not in a popularity contest. Be prepared for your child to reject you. He or she will most likely come around later.

This article was originally published in Psychology Today *online. Psychologist Jeffrey Bernstein, PhD, is the author of* Ten Days to a Less Defiant Child, The Stress Survival Guide for Teens *and* Mindfulness for Teen Worry. *He can be reached at www. drjeffonline.com.*

Hello, Anybody Out There?

Whole books have been written about the best ways to talk to your adult children. Deborah Tannen, in particular, is known for *You're Wearing THAT? Understanding Mothers and Daughters in Conversation* and *I Only Say This Because I Love You: How the way we Talk Can Make or Break Family Relationships Throughout our Lives.* And then there is the avalanche of online articles with such titles as, "Six Things Your Should Never Say to your Grown Child, " "How to Talk WITH—not AT—your Adult Children," and "Hints for Communicating with Adult Children."

They're not responding

But many parents never get the chance to talk to their adult children—diplomatically or otherwise—because their offspring simply don't return their calls. Or texts. Or emails. For every daughter who speaks to her mother daily, there seem to be a hundred who are basically incommunicado. And these are not the estrangement situations! The younger generation's lack of responsiveness is a major, major sore spot with parents, one that leaves them feeling frustrated, hurt, and angry. "He only calls when he needs something," "It's so hard to make plans when she doesn't respond," and "When my friends ask, 'What are the kids up to?' I have to make up some vague answer." It's ironic that just when we have so many ways to stay in touch, silence ensues.

Do the rules of civility no longer apply to grown offspring or have the rules changed radically? According to psychotherapist Elizabeth Wolfson, PhD, it is both. "As a parent, you are still your children's one and only, and perhaps for that reason they feel they can be more casual/careless, less polite, in their communications with you. It's likely you are with them as well. But it also true that texting has changed everything and the old rules of engagement no longer apply.

It's a generational thing

"Anyone under the age of 35 is texting not phoning or even emailing," according to Dr. Wolfson. "Moreover, this form of communication has thrown out all the pleasantries, such as please, thank you, a sign-off, or even a signature. And according to the rules of texting, no answer simply means the recipient is busy. It's not a referendum on your relationship. While to you not getting a response, let alone a timely one, be may be unbearably rude; to your offspring it's an accepted aspect of the medium. You may yearn for what you think of as human contact—to them texting is human contact."

To get a grip on your feelings, you might want to recite the Serenity Prayer below or, if you still want to hear a real voice, phone your realtor. She'll call you back.

> *God grant me the serenity*
> *to accept the things I cannot change;*
> *courage to change the things I can;*
> *and wisdom to know the difference.*

Communicating Today

In my previousarticle on the topic of intergenerational communications—or lack thereof—I examined how today's grown offspring have a whole different attitude toward staying in touch. Here, I discuss how to work with it.

According to psychotherapist Elizabeth Wolfson, PhD, "Be as open-minded and nonjudgmental as possible. Take the 'client-centered' approach: 'It's your world and I'm merely stepping into it.' One way to practice that is by speaking your grown offspring's language, and today that language is a lot more visual. Shots of everyday activities that you might once have considered banal are now keeping family life alive, so start snapping and transmitting. You'll also want to become familiar with Instagram, resend from Pinterest, and load up on the latest apps that loom so large in your adult child's life.

Keep it short and visual

If communications are now a lot more visual, they are also a lot shorter. Expressing yourself in 140 characters may not be satisfying but it's what's happening. To move beyond the old acronyms, such as *LOL*, get a book or a 12-year-old so you can dazzle your adult children with how hip you are. And ask their advice on your personal hash tag. To see what their adult children are up to, some parents swear by Facebook. They "Comment," "Like," and "Friend," to their heart's content. Other parents consider going on their offspring's pages spying or crossing a boundary and refuse to do it.

Still other parents stay in touch via the old-fashioned

phone call, sometimes bringing it into modern times through Skype or Facetime. For some of them, a weekly call is the glue that holds their relationship together. "If you want to go that route," advises Dr. Wolfson, "Ask for it in a way that demonstrates respect, for example, 'How would it be if we had a set date to talk?' That's likely to go over a lot better than, 'You never call me and at least this way I'll hear your voice once a week.' If your goal is to keep the lines of communication open, inducing guilt may produce the opposite effect."

Reader's Comment

I am divorced and live alone. I like to hear the voice of my only daughter, but she is careless about returning my calls—or texts or emails. I know that her job keeps her very busy, but I can't help feeling slighted. To find out what she's up to, I am reduced to checking her Facebook page, an action I prefer not to think of as spying. M.M.

Learning the Boundaries of Communication

by Donne Davis

When it comes to communicating with your adult children, where do you get stuck? I posed this question to members of the GaGa Sisterhood recently and added, is it around discipline, visitation, values or boundaries? All of the above, and more, they answered. One member said: "All I have to do is open my mouth and my son misinterprets what I'm saying." Another joked: "OMG! Just asking 'how are you' can trigger a reaction. Even though we have a lovely relationship, my daughter is very sensitive!"

The civilized conversation

Of all the challenges we grandmas face, the biggest seems to be around communication. It's not surprising. Miscommunication or misunderstanding is the number one reason why so many tough conversations escalate to uncomfortable levels of tension, resentment or lack of trust. How can we share our feelings and perspectives with our children and be heard without causing hurt, anger or silence? How can we have a close relationship with our children if we avoid meaningful conversation? These questions pose some of our biggest challenges as parents.

Communication with adult children takes sensitivity, empathy, patience and a lot of practice. According to Ruth Nemzoff, author of *Don't Bite Your Tongue: How to Foster Rewarding Relationships with your Adult*

Children, relationships with our children can feel more like relationships with a spouse or lover than a friend. They share the same intensity and ability to evoke anger, joy, heartbreak, embarrassment, or pride. The speaker at our GaGa Sisterhood meeting, Catherine Morris, MFT, agrees. In her psychotherapy practice, she helps couples understand how words can trigger feelings we often can't see or get in touch with. It's the same with parents and adult children; we often have old patterns we fall into when talking to each other. We have automatic reactions to each other's behavior that trigger more reactions and we get caught in negative cycles.

Morris uses techniques based on Emotionally Focused Therapy, developed by Sue Johnson, author of *Hold Me Tight: Seven Conversations for a Lifetime of Love.* Johnson has taught thousands of therapists how to create more secure emotional bonds between couples. You create trust in a relationship when both people feel emotionally safe and feel comfortable being vulnerable and asking for what they need.

Understanding each other

With our children, as with our spouses, we can have the same arguments in countless forms over the years. The complexity of the relationship—investments of time, money and energy over the years, involvement in their successes and failures—all contribute to a delicate dance that must be developed over time and not always with successful outcomes. We must each learn the boundaries of communication and remember that even though we raised them, they are now adults raising their own children and often with very different parenting strategies than ours.

The first step in any communication is to understand each other. Morris suggests that when we get stuck in a conversation and notice we're getting a "look" or resistance from our child, we need to take a breath and try to clarify what we heard by using phrases like: *I want to understand; I'm confused; I want to be clear; can you help me understand how to say it?* If her response is, *"I don't want to talk about it,"* then you can say: *"I respect that and I'm wondering if you might help me understand why you don't want to talk about it."*

We also need to examine our true intentions when we talk to our children. If we're trying to change their behavior or thinking, we're going to get in trouble and most likely be met with a wall of resistance. But if we sincerely want to understand their viewpoint and lead with genuine curiosity, we'll stand a better chance of a mutually respectful exchange.

Strategies to Use When Talking to Adult Children

- Be curious
- Listen without being "judgy"
- Understand what triggers emotions
- Listen without fixing
- Take a breath before reacting and calm down
- Step away; take a time out
- Make "I" statements rather than "you always"
- Use phrases like:

  Help me understand why you don't want to talk about it.

  Can you help me understand how to say it?

Did I hear you say ...

I'm confused, I want to be clear.

What just went wrong?

This is just me being your mother

For more wisdom on communicating with adult children, read Ruth Nemzoff's *11 Tips for Communicating.*

Donne Davis is the founder of GaGa Sisterhood and author of When Being a Grandma Isn't So Grand: 4 Keys to L.O.V.E. Your Grandchild's Parents.

3 Ways to Get Closer to Your Adult Child

by Jeffrey Bernstein, PhD

Many parents of adult children yearn to feel more connected to them. In the following examples (names changed to protect confidentiality) from my parent coaching work, you will find tips to feel closer to your adult child:

1. Think "less is more." Barbara made the mistake of thinking her newly graduated, twenty-three-year-old son, Kyle, was willing to be as available as he had previously been, to speak on the phone or respond to her texts. Much to her dismay, his text response time and phone availability became less upon graduating college and moving on with a new job.

Barbara longed for the days when Kyle lived at home and they'd have those cool, "What's the meaning of life?" conversations. She always felt like a close, connected mom, and prided herself on Kyle's past quick responses to her texts and calls. Once Kyle had moved away to take his new job, Barbara wrongly anticipated that he'd lean on her and she'd get frequent updates how he was doing.

Solution: It helped Barbara to realize that "less is more." In other words, she became aware that not having daily contact was okay. Less contact did not mean Kyle was detached. Interestingly, as Barbara let go and backed off, she began hearing more from Kyle.

2. Don't go guilting. Alice, had some strong feelings about where her adult son, Larry, should spend his time for the holidays. Breaking with past years of every Christmas spent at home, Larry enthusiastically opted to go to his girlfriend's family home for the holiday. Alice initially tried to leverage Larry with guilt. ("We never get to see you, why can't you and your girlfriend come out our way. Grandma will be with us and she may not be around much longer.") As you can imagine, Barbara's coaxing did not go over well.

Solution: Alice subsequently reflected on her overstep, owned it, and apologized to Larry. She had wisely realized that Larry did not have to be at her home for Christmas. She further saw that supporting Larry's happiness at his girlfriend's house could give her a deep sense of fulfillment

Larry felt relieved of guilt from Barbara after she apologized to him and then made plans to stop by and see her the day after Christmas. This example shows that slinging guilt when you expect your adult children to be available will be interpreted as an unfair burden. But when your happiness doesn't entirely depend on your children having to be with you, you will not likely fall into the guilting trap.

3. Remember your child is a grown-up. Unless your advice is solicited, try not to impose it on your grown child. If you say infantilizing things like, "Why are you still eating candy?" it may be taken as you being too intrusive. The bottom line: Gently expose your concerns without imposing them.

Solution: What you could say in the above example is, "You certainly get to make your own decisions about what to eat. I know you enjoy it, but you may want to consider, if you have not already, eating that candy in moderation.

But that is up to you. I appreciate you hearing me on this."
Some parents may feel this type of response is weak. If you
do, that is okay. But I never have adult children complain
to me about sensitively delivered caring messages from their
parents!

This article was originally published in Psychology Today *online.*
Psychologist Jeffrey Bernstein, PhD, is the author of Ten Days
to a Less Defiant Child, The Stress Survival Guide for Teens
and Mindfulness for Teen Worry. *He can be reached at www.*
drjeffonline.com.

Reader's Comment

"I went to visit my middle daughter after she had just
given birth to her first child. In the shared glow of
the newborn baby, I experienced a closeness with her
that I hadn't felt in years. This is as good as it gets, I
thought and on the spot I vowed to work harder at our
relationship. It's been six months and so far, so good."
D.B.

Too Close for Comfort?

Todd *grew up in a tiny Michigan town, population 7,500. Although now living on the East Coast, he returns a few times a year to visit old friends and family. Recently, he decided to buy a vacation home in the town, which happened to be a half-mile from the home of his daughter, Lisa.*

After hearing that he would be down the road, Lisa flipped out, accusing him of wanting to spy on her, cramp her style, and take her children away from their scheduled activities to be with him. Her tirade left Todd shocked and hurt—especially since he had just built a tool shed for her. What should Todd do?

- *Withdraw his offer on the vacation house?*

- *Reach out again to Lisa to explain that her upscale neighborhood is really the only game in town?*

- *Go ahead with his plans despite her hostility?*

The Panel Weighs In:

Jim: *Todd should go ahead but work at reestablishing his relationship with Lisa.*

Carla: *He should go ahead while letting Lisa know that he will make appointments to see the kids, and will never just drop in.*

Cathy: *Lisa's reaction is understandable; everyone wants his or her own space. Todd should look for another property—on the other side of town.*

Stan: *The first thing he should do is dismantle that tool shed!*

Short-Distance Love

A lot has been written about how to stay in touch when you live far from your adult children, but little has been written about how to make it work when you live nearby. To find out I spoke with several parents and grown children who live close to one another and found they drew great warmth, comfort, and companionship from the situation. Here is what they had to say:

Presence makes the heart grow fonder

All the parents I spoke with insisted that they would be as emotionally close to their kids if they were physically far away, but being in the same town or reasonable driving distance was so much more satisfying. Differences can be smoothed over faster and more effectively face-to-face than through electronic devices. And with repeated contact comes closeness.

- As one man said of the son who does his legal work, "I know we could do all our business over the phone, but our lunches are the highlight of my week."

- For the kids who come back to the place where they grew up, the familiar environment seems to be the draw. But one mother opined, "My daughter took a look at her two decrepit parents and probably thought, "How many years have they got left? They'll need me."

- According to a member of the younger generation, "In some ways it's easier having my parents close by because the visits can be so much more natural, spontaneous, and shorter. When we lived apart we had to cram all these activities into a short period of time, and it felt so much more pressured and artificial."

- Said another young man of his father, "We both have some kind of internal alarm clock that goes off when we haven't seen each other for a few days. Then we'll take the dogs for a walk or meet for a cup of coffee. I can't say we have any set rituals, but we do manage to see each other fairly often."

- "She's spontaneous and I'm a planner," volunteered one parent whose daughter just moved a few blocks away. "But I'm trying to loosen up and she's trying to plan ahead because otherwise we'll never connect."

Please include me—on my terms

When grandchildren are involved, making arrangements becomes even more complicated, but grandparents will move heaven and earth to be with their children's children. They know that their peers would give their eyeteeth to have the grandchildren close by. Sometimes, though, they could do with less togetherness.

- "Babysitting is not what I do, it's not who I am," one grandma told me. "Other women love to cluck, bake, and fuss, but it's just not my thing. I know this is a disappointment to my son, but my first priority now is my husband, his stepfather."

- "They expect me to be at every recital, soccer game, and birthday party," lamented a grandfather. "If I hesitate to commit, I can hear the unspoken reproach, 'Well, what else do you have to do with your time?' I say yes because otherwise I'd feel guilty, but sometimes I'd just as soon stay home and get the executive report later."

"I'm my own person!" was a refrain I heard time and again from parents. They were proud of the fact that their adult children didn't consider them a burden.

- "My daughter rarely asks me to sleep over, which, if I am perfectly truthful, is fine with me," one father told me. 'My' room in her house is actually the storeroom, and I'd rather sleep in my own bed."

On the other hand, additional attention would be flattering. "I'm glad my kids know I'm self-sufficient. Still, I wouldn't mind if they worried about me a little more!" one divorcee confessed.

The spouse factor

When two generations live in the same town, spouses have to be considered.

- As one young woman said, "We do things as a family, but I would say I see my mom more often on my own. You shouldn't try to do everything all together—it's too much."

- Another chimed in, "You have to have frank discussions with your husband about the relationship when your folks are nearby because he didn't grow up in your home. Things you don't see, brush off, don't bother you, or seem natural may grate on him or seem downright weird. Also, he might resent your closeness to your folks if his are far away, emotionally or physically."

To sum up, there's no doubt that parents and grown children who choose to live near one other are a self-selected group. Nevertheless, their caring and closeness are heartwarming compared to the rancor I see in so many adult families today.

- "We have such a good time together," was a refrain I heard again and again from my interviewees.

- "Aside from the mother/daughter thing, we are friends," several said, not without a little surprise.

- And finally, "I have lived far away as well as close by my parents," one grown daughter reflected. "Living close by is not without its challenges, but at the end of the day I'd have to say it's definitely a net plus."

Reader's Comment

In "Short-Distance Love" one can see the generational benefits of proximity. Living at a distance from my children, it takes an effort to meet, and we get only rare glimpses of ordinary life. On the other hand, distance allows for unparalleled growth and maturation. P.D.

Chapter 7

Special Situations

This chapter is a tribute to parents who try to do their best for their adult children in the face of severe obstacles. I start with addictions, which are such a scourge on family life today that I devote three articles to various facets of the problem. The emphasis here is on ways parents can cope when drug or alcohol addiction hits home.

Next, I cover one result of millennials' changing attitude toward marriage. With fully a quarter of them thinking of skipping it entirely, many of their parents are left with no grandchildren or grandchildren born out of wedlock. Then I ask, "Who Pays for What on a Family Vacation?" I got many heated responses from readers who have been grappling with this sticky dilemma in their own lives.

I also include articles on parenting intellectually challenged children who age out of public services and the effect on a family when a father dies young. I conclude the chapter with a discussion of anorexia, a particular menace for young adult women in our society, and a moving tribute by a mother to her remarkable daughter, who fell victim to the disease and ultimately decided not to fight it.

Drug Addiction, Part 1:
A National Scourge

In the last 17 years there's been a 300 percent increase in fatal overdoses from drugs, many of them prescription pain relievers called opioids—and that's just the tip of the iceberg. Right now more than twenty million people in the United States are suffering from drug abuse disorders, including ingestion of heroin, the cheaper and more readily available street sister of prescription drugs.

More deadly than traffic accidents

Opioid abuse accounts for one and a half more deaths per year than vehicular accidents. Moreover, it's an equal opportunity destroyer that afflicts the middle-class, the well-educated, and the well-loved as well as the downtrodden, the high school dropout, and the neglected. Given the epic proportions of this scourge, it may very well have ensnared your adult child, too.

What's the tipoff? If you pay attention, you will probably notice troubling changes: Your daughter may have lost weight, started to argue with her siblings, become neglectful of her appearance and careless with her possessions. If she's still in school, her grades may have slipped and if she works, she may be having trouble holding onto a job. Her friends are less savory and you are less likely to be introduced to them.

Taking the first step

What's a parent to do? According to Maureen Murdock, PhD, a psychotherapist who has written widely on the issue of mental illness and substance abuse, "The first step is accepting the fact that addiction is a disease, one that often runs in families. It shouldn't be a moral issue, but parents feel so much shame and guilt when the subject comes up that their first response is often incredulity and denial, not to mention outrage: 'That's impossible!' they'll say. 'My son has always been a good kid.'"

After you come to grips with the reality of the situation yourself, get your spouse onboard if you have a spouse. Dr. Murdock says that when parents are not on the same page—which is often the case—the long road to recovery becomes that much longer. To prevent a drug abusing adult child from playing one parent off against the other, she urges you to do whatever you need to do, including couples therapy, to present a united front.

Remember, says Dr. Murdock:

- You didn't cause it
- You can't control it
- You can't cure it

For information on treatment and other options, you can contact the Hazelden Betty Ford Foundation at 1-866-275-2213 or *hazeldenbettyford.org*. You might also want to read *Addict in the Family: Stories of Loss, Hope, and Recovery* by Beverly Conyers, a book highly recommended by Dr. Murdock.

Drug Addiction, Part 2: Acknowledging

In our first article about an adult child's substance abuse problem, we discussed the symptoms of addiction and the need to see it for what it is: a disease. Here, we'll explore how to engage your son or daughter who is using. It's scary to contemplate breaking the code of silence that so often surrounds the loaded subject of addiction. Rather than risk alienating their child for good, parents will pretend nothing's amiss. That's the worse thing you could do, according to Dr. Maureen Murdock, a psychotherapist who has written widely on the issue of mental illness and substance abuse, "You must speak up because either it's the end of your relationship or the end of your child's life. The choice is clear: there is no choice."

False starts are likely

Dr. Murdock emphasizes that there will be several conversations and likely several false starts before your child is open to receiving treatment. Still, the key thing is to begin. You and other members of the family should be coached by an addiction specialist or have that person in the room, if possible. Dr. Murdock urges you to address your child as neutrally and nonjudgmentally as possible. If you get angry and start blaming, the intervention won't be productive. No matter what your actual words, project a message that the family is caring, loving, and there for her:

- We are concerned about your behavior;
- We suspect you're using drugs;

- This can't continue. You are comprising your health, possibly fatally, by your risky behavior;

- We're worried and we want you to get help.

Your child will most likely minimize his addiction if he acknowledges it at all. According to Dr. Murdock, those who abuse substances have a distorted perception that all is okay. "It's such a small amount," they'll say. "I'm only using periodically," "It's your problem, not mine," and "How could you think this of me!" Those who abuse substances are in denial and that denial is very strong and difficult to overcome. Further complicating the issue is the fact your adult child is not a minor; you can't order him to get treatment.

How does your child feel?

Dr. Murdock says the key is to hear your child out. Encourage her to talk about her feelings. Perhaps she's been lonely, bullied, unpopular, depressed or unbearably pressured by her peers. Perhaps she's actually bipolar or on sensory overload. To combat mental illness or social anxiety, she may think, "Ah, drugs will make me cool."

Dr. Murdock stresses that there are no magic bullets and no shortcuts on the road to recovery. No matter how you slice it, it's a long, slow, painful process, but by getting the subject out in the open, at least you're making a start. In part 3 of this series, we'll look at things you can do to help your child and keep your sanity as the journey continues.

Drug Addiction, Part 3: Detaching

At the same time you are identifying your adult child's substance abuse, confronting him, and getting him into treatment, you need to be paying attention to yourself. It's hard not to get sucked into the 24/7 drama that is addiction. As the "strong one" you find yourself being hyper-vigilant, forever waiting for the next relapse or disaster, always on high alert should you need to don your Superman cape and swing into action. Despite the best of intentions, your child's struggle with drugs becomes your struggle until all boundaries are gone and healthy caregiving deteriorates into co-dependency.

Although it seems counterintuitive, stepping away is key, says Beverly Conyers,* in her article for the Hazeldon Betty Ford Foundation, *"Eight Reasons Why Detaching with Love is Good for your Addicted Loved One."*

- Detachment lets fresh air into your relationship. If you're involved with a substance abuser, chances are your relationship has become unhealthy.

- Detachment allows abusers to face the consequences of their choices. Most of us have to learn from experience, including addicts, which make life experiences so much more impactful than warnings.

- Detachment saves abusers from the harmful effects of enabling. When we do for them what they could and should do for themselves, we're keeping our loved ones perpetually dependent and immature.

- Detachment empowers the abuser to behave like an adult. Addicts tend to get stuck at the age they were when they started using. Detaching gives them the opportunity to develop inner resources.

- Detachment allows abusers to experience the satisfaction that comes from personal accomplishment. If we're over-involved, when things go well it's our accomplishment. When things go wrong it's our fault.

- Detachment reduces the shame our addicted loved ones feel about themselves. By detaching from our expectations of them and allowing them to find their own way, we stop contributing to their self-loathing.

- Detachment is an expression of love. Neither a selfish act nor an admission of failure, detaching with love states that we believe the substance abuser has the inner strength and intelligence to make it. As Conyers says, "What could be more loving than that?"

Beverly Conyers is the author of Addict in the Family: Stories of Loss, Hope and Recovery. *She began writing about addiction when she discovered that her youngest daughter was addicted to heroin. She is convinced that, "There is no such thing as a hopeless case. Everything can change even when we least expect it, and the miracle of recovery happens every day."*

One Drink Too Many

John and Katrina think their 31-year-old daughter, Melissa, has a drinking problem. She may not be a full-on alcoholic—yet—but she's coming in late to work, hanging out with scruffy characters, letting her hygiene go, ordering cocktails at lunch, and even nodding off at the dinner table. What should Melissa's parents do?

- *Wait until she hits rock bottom and then get her into rehab?*

- *Join a group for parents of alcoholics?*

- *Say they're going on the wagon for health reasons and ask her to join them?*

The Panel Weighs In:

Susan: *AA tells parents to go to Alanon, where they'll get the direction, tools, and support they need. They will also learn how to stage a successful family intervention guided by a professional therapist.*

Tony: *Saying they're going on the wagon is not authentic. Waiting until she hits rock bottom is chancy at best; she could die or drive drunk. They need to have a frank talk with Melissa NOW.*

Nancy: *I don't think it's so bad to go on the wagon as a show of solidarity. At least you feel you're doing something and your child knows she's not alone.*

James: *Detach, detach, detach! The parents can't make Melissa's failure their failure or three lives will wind up being ruined, not just one.*

My Son-in-Law Has No Ambition

Even as a teenager Maggie's daughter, Lizzie, always brought home "strays," those boys who would never amount to anything. She was a born rescuer. Despite her parents' repeated warnings, she eventually married one of these unpromising fellows, Mike, and their predictions came true: she works, he doesn't. Mike's behavior might have been defensible when their only child was a baby and he was the nanny, but now that "baby" is in elementary school and Mike is still hanging around the house.

It's driving Maggie's husband, Eddie, nuts because to him a husband is the breadwinner, period. Eddie has been telling Lizzie to dump Mike for ten years, and, while Maggie sees his point, she's afraid to lose her over this. Maggie feels caught in the middle between father and daughter. Should she:

- Diplomatically tell her husband to sit down and zip it because that train has left the station?

- Work through Lizzie to urge Mike to find some kind of work, any work, to appease his father-in-law?

- Accept the situation as it is and just let Eddie vent?

The Panel Weighs In:

Our panelists had extremely strong—and diametrically opposed—feelings about this situation:

Peter: Eddie has to keep his mouth shut because his daughter is an adult, and he needs to be supportive of her decision. He is totally wrong and needs therapy *to stop his stupid behavior. He's got to live with the situation—silently—even if it sticks in his craw.*

Joyce: *I think Eddie is right. Mike is mooching off his wife and it's despicable. He's a loser. Eddie should take the younger man out to lunch without the women and read him the riot act. Then he should tell his daughter to open a separate checking account and, if he's subsidizing them, only pay into that account.*

Rob: *Eddie has to let live and let go. If Lizzie and Mike have an understanding that is working for them, he has to respect that. This generation has a different idea of gender-related roles. However, if Eddie is enabling the situation by giving the kids money, he's justified in making the allowance contingent upon his son-in-law working.*

Kathy: *Eddie is giving Lizzie good advice, but the four of them need to go into therapy together to lessen the tension and accept that Mike is never going to change. Maggie needs to keep her eyes on the prize, though, which is an ongoing relationship with her daughter and grandchild while sympathizing with her husband. Not easy but necessary!*

Readers' Comments

I don't think it matters which parent is the one who is the "stay-at-home." If a family can afford to have only one parent work outside of the house and have one at home, that's a lot better than hiring multiple someones to do all the things that the "house husband" does: cooks meals; cleans the house; chauffeurs the kid(s) to/from school, extra-curricular activities, doctor & dental appointments etc; cares for the kid(s) when they are home sick and on vacation; does the grocery shopping; as well as household repairs and a myriad of other mundane tasks. In fact, the family might not even be able to afford to pay all the folks they'd have to hire to fill all of those positions if both parents worked full time out of the house! P.J.

This is a delicate issue and if the parents press the "loser" husband it could cause friction, unease, and perhaps estrangement. The latter must be avoided. I'm sure the daughter realizes her situation and, for whatever reason, has chosen to accept it. For her it is preferable to being lonely and raising a family alone. Reminding her of this less-than-ideal situation is kind of like calling attention to one's overweight adult child. He/she knows it! The daughter has accepted her (for us) unorthodox husband and it's time for the parents to also. B.H.

Hand Up or Hand Out?

Betsy and Gino's son-in-law of eight years, Alfie, wants to open a restaurant, but he doesn't have enough income to qualify for the loan that would make it happen. Now Alfie is asking his in-laws to be co-signers on the loan, and they don't know what to do. The argument against is that restaurants are an iffy proposition at best and Alfie is neither an experienced restaurateur nor an experienced entrepreneur. If the restaurant doesn't make it, Betsy and Gino would be on the hook for the remainder of the loan, which would make their retirement a whole lot less comfortable. The argument for is that their daughter is pressuring them to help her husband realize his dream, and they worry she'll hold it against them if they say no.

- Should Betsy and Gino follow their head and adhere to Benjamin Franklin's famous edict, "Neither a borrower nor a lender be?"
- Should they follow their heart and help out the young couple?
- Should they be full partners in the business with Alfie?

The Panel Weighs In:

Parker: I'm a soft touch, so I would give Alfie the loan. It's my daughter's future we're talking about here, after all. However, I would attach lots of strings to the loan, such as insisting Alfie go through small business training.

Louise: No, no, no! This is a lark. If Alfie were serious

about the new venture, he would have apprenticed at a restaurant and saved up for his new business. I would risk my daughter's estrangement rather than put my own retirement in jeopardy.

Rob: *Betsy and Gino are damned if they do and damned if they don't. I guess I'd give the kids some money but not so much that it jeopardizes my own future.*

Franny: *Oh, why couldn't the kids have asked Alfie's parents, instead? His request puts Gino and Betsy in such an awkward position. Ultimately, they should turn him down rather than become his business partner and banker—a sure recipe for disaster.*

Baby Out of Wedlock and Into the Family

Of all the changes to which Baby Boomers have had to adjust in recent decades, none has been more revolutionary than the meteoric rise of out-of-wedlock babies. Fifty years ago only 10 percent of births in America were to unmarried women; by 2017 that figure had skyrocketed to 40 percent for women who were either solo or cohabitating. By now we all know a family that has had this experience and that family may very well be our own.

What happened to cause this monumental shift?

According to some researchers, the end of shotgun marriages was the main driver. They say that until the early 1970s, the shotgun marriage was the norm in premarital sexual relations. As one man said, "If a girl gets pregnant you married her. There wasn't no choice. So I married her."

Others say it was the decline of the stigma of unwed motherhood. This transformation in attitudes was captured by *The New York Times*: "In the 'old days' of the 1960s, '50s, and '40s, pregnant teenagers were pariahs, banished from schools, ostracized by their peers or scurried out of town to give birth in secret." Today they are "supported and embraced in their decision to give birth, keep their babies, continue their education, and participate in school activities."

Still others contend, although it seems counterintuitive, that it was the availability of the birth control pill and legalized abortion. Becoming pregnant no longer meant you were a "bad girl," because everyone was doing it.

Moreover, with movie stars bragging about giving birth to a "love child," young women now had role models for keeping their illegitimate offspring.

Who is having babies out of wedlock

Those most responsible for the dramatic increase in of out-of-wedlock babies are white women. Their rate of nonmarital births has nearly tripled since 1980, the fastest of any ethnic group. The group ranges from young, poor, uneducated women who are living with a boyfriend or their parents to older, highly successful career women who feel it's their last chance to have a child. Government statistics don't track how many unwed women are mothers by choice, but there is evidence their numbers are substantial. California Cryobank, one of the major sperm banks in the U.S., says about a third of its clients are single mothers by choice, and this figure is increasing

With so many young people getting married later or not marrying at all, cohabitators loom ever larger as procreators. In 1997, the first year for which data on cohabitation are available, 20 percent of unmarried parents who lived with their children were also living with a partner. Since that time, their share has risen to 35 percent. One thing has not changed, though: solo parents remain overwhelmingly female. The percentage of unmarried parents who are solo fathers has held steady at 12 percent.

Throughout America, the average age of unmarried moms is 21. Teen pregnancies everywhere are down dramatically, dropping in Philadelphia alone from 2,525 to just 126 between 2005 and 2017, according to census figures. Experts say that high school sex education and the Affordable Care Act, which has increased the supply of contraceptives, deserve the credit.

The United States is by no means the only country experiencing a dramatic increase in out-of-wedlock births. In 2016 of the world's 140 million births, about 15 percent —or 21 million—occurred out of wedlock. There are major differences, though, from society to society. In about 25 countries, including China, India and much of Africa, the proportion of such births is typically around 1 percent. In another 25 countries, mostly in Latin America, it is more than 60 percent, and this represents a big jump from just 50 years ago.

Accepted but not applauded

Many Americans view the increase in unmarried parenthood—solo mothering especially—as a negative trend for society. In a Pew Research Center survey, two-thirds of adults said that more single women raising children on their own was bad for society, and 48 percent said the same about more unmarried couples raising children. Older Americans and those with higher levels of education were especially likely to view these trends as bad for society.

Even so, other data suggest a slight uptick in acceptance. In 1994, 35 percent of adults agreed or strongly agreed that single parents could raise children as well as two married parents, according to data from the General Social Survey; by 2012 those in agreement had risen to 48 percent.

Love it or hate it, we all need to adjust to it because— given the trend toward single parenting and cohabitation— the out-of-wedlock family member is here to stay.

Who Pays for What on a Family Vacation?

The Christmas holidays are fast approaching, and Lila and George would like to rent a cabin at a ski resort for the whole family, which includes three 30-something children and two spouses. Everyone would have to fly up, and their single son, Paul, is struggling financially. Their daughters and sons-in-law are doing much better. Lila and George are retirees who are barely making it themselves.

- Should Lila and George underwrite Paul's airfare but expect the other two families to pay their own way?

- Are the parents entirely responsible for the cost of the cabin?

- Who picks up the bill for food?

- Would your answers be different if Lila and George were wealthy?

The Panel Weighs In:

There was a lot of heat around this issue. As one of the panelists said, "You're describing my life!" They all agreed, though, that their answers would be different if Lila and George had a lot of money.

Foster: When parents can't afford it, they shouldn't try to bribe their adult children to be with them at the holidays by offering a ski vacation. However, if the kids are enthusiastic about the prospect, then everyone should pay his or her own way and the more well-to-

do sibs should subsidize their brother.

Steven: *It's not a bribe! Memories are important and vacations put everyone in different "fun" places. The family should problem-solve to try to make it happen. However, everyone needs to have some "skin in the game." Even if Paul can't pay full freight, he should pay something, such as being responsible for one day of food.*

Nan: *The point is for the family to be together at Christmas not to show off on Facebook where they've been. Taking the whole crew away for the holidays has been glamorized, but it doesn't seem so glamorous when the credit card charges show up. If the family does go, they should divvy up the costs of the cabin and the food.*

Wilhelmina: *Even though it's embarrassing to discuss money, it's better to get the financial arrangements settled ahead of time rather than harbor resentments. No one wants to feel he's paying more than he's comfortable with or more than his fair share. That would create tensions among the siblings and ruin the vacation before it even starts!*

Parenting the Intellectually Challenged Adult Child

Everything gets more complicated as a special needs child ages. When he turns 22 he will age out of all the public school services to which he has been entitled. At the same time his caregivers—and those are usually his parents—are getting older, too. In Illinois alone there are more than 30,000 people with disabilities living with caregivers 60 or older. Multiply that by the number of states in the union, and you see the magnitude of the situation.

Solely responsible

Jeannette P. is one of those statistics. Jeannette is a 63-year-old single parent whose developmentally challenged son, Joey, will turn 22 in September. At that point Jeannette will have to add "chauffer" to her long list of duties as Joey will no longer be allowed to take the school bus, or attend his special program at a nearby community college. Jeannette will then be solely responsible for arranging her son's volunteer work, socialization, and recreation. Although Joey is eager to use the public bus, Jeannette is afraid that he would get panicky if he debarks at the wrong stop or is harassed by other riders. It won't be easy to juggle everything as Jeannette has to work to keep the family afloat. While she gets some compensation from the government, it's not enough to live on.

Joey's impending milestone reminds Jeannette that she better hurry up and get a trust in place before she has a health crisis that will prevent her from caring for her son. She is also on the hunt for a small group home, which she sees this as the next step in his life's journey. A small group home would provide a structured schedule, mealtime preparation, transportation and, according to Jeannette, "A chance for Joey to be all he can be." Unfortunately, such ideal living situations are hard to find and the list to get into them is long. Some parents are so frustrated by the wait that they are even seeking to turn their own homes into group living situations.

In the meantime, like most principal caregivers, Jeannette is mentally and physically exhausted from the strain of caring for her son 24/7. "More often than not I feel helpless," she says. The government is of little help. Of the roughly 220,000 Illinoisans with disabilities, for example, fewer than 28,000 are receiving services from the state. Working in isolation, with no specialized training, little support, and meager psychic return, caregivers are at wit's end. A caregiver support group can provide some solace. Here, the Jeannettes of the community speak frankly about the isolation their children face, their kids' medical, mental and developmental needs, and the money it takes to provide for it all. They get answers to their questions from the experts, but the real value is hearing from other parents whose testimony validates their own concerns and deepest fears.

Finding solace in a support group

The future is never far from these parents' minds. Says Jeannette, "As I would with any child, I want to keep my son moving forward. The key is finding the right place for Joey. Wherever he lands up, I want him to feel safe, happy, and supported. That's when I'll finally be able to draw a deep breath, knowing that even without me, he'll be okay."

The Ragged Edge

For months now Jim's daughter, Cara, has been either a whirling dervish or a weeping basket case. Jim is concerned that she has bipolar disorder and wants her to seek help, but he's unsure how to proceed. Cara has gotten very defensive when he's suggested therapy in the past, and he doesn't want to jeopardize their tenuous relationship. He'd also like to talk it over with her new husband, who seems oblivious, but Jim doesn't want to throw a monkey wrench into their marriage, either.

- *Should Jim take the risk and confront Cara directly?*
- *Should he feel out her husband?*
- *Should he trust that since she's a grownup, she'll go into treatment when she's ready?*
- *Should he seek professional guidance himself?*

The Panel Weighs In:

The panel was all in favor of Jim seeking professional guidance. Where they differed, though, was how he should go about it.

Lila. *Jim should go to a therapist—with Cara in tow. It's too hard for anyone struggling with mental illness to take that first step alone. Yes, the father/daughter relationship may be rocky for a while, but it's a risk Jim has to take if he's to help her get well.*

Chase. *Forget Cara's husband, who sounds like he's out to lunch, and forget the idea of Cara seeking treatment on her own because, since she hasn't done it* *yet, she probably won't do it now. It's up to Jim to stage an intervention to get his daughter the professional care she needs.*

Maxine. *I read that 1 in 6 Americans experiences mental health issues each year, yet there's still so much stigma and shame attached to these disorders. Jim has to tread carefully with Cara, who may be more fragile than he realizes, but he can't waver in his goal of getting her into treatment. Her life may depend on it.*

Peter. *Jim should go into therapy first to find out how to deal with the situation. Then, if Cara won't join him, at least he's helping himself.*

Reader's Comment

My immediate reaction is to the word "confront." I think in any healthy parent-adult child relationship, we need to think of each other as supportive and caring. That would be the tone this father should take - not confronting. He could suggest they get together someplace quiet for coffee and just start a conversation by asking how things have been going lately. Let his daughter know he cares about her and that it seems like she's having a rough time. After she's had a chance to talk about her feelings, let her husband offer his perspective on how things have been. Then it's the father's turn—after he's listened without interrupting and shown empathy for his daughter—to say that he cares about her and wants her to know that he's there for her. How can he support her during this time? Maybe by talking about options and resources, they'll be able to start addressing the key issues. D.D.

Could It Really Be All My Fault?

Cynthia's son, Daniel, has been at home for a year after dropping out of college. He refuses to help out around the house, works only a few hours a week at menial jobs, and is extremely belligerent toward his mother. Daniel's therapist asked Cynthia to come in for joint counseling, and now she's enduring hours of accusations that everything that's gone wrong in Daniel's life is her fault. It's making her a nervous wreck.

- Should Cynthia sit there and take it in hopes it will help Daniel get well?
- Should she try to explain and defend her behavior during his childhood?
- Should she refuse to attend any more of these therapy sessions?

The Panel Weighs In:

Thad: There are definitely boundary issues here. At home Cynthia has to set limits on Daniel's behavior, and in therapy she has to start speaking up for herself. Letting him wallow in victimhood and playing on her guilt is getting neither of them anywhere.

Wendy: Cynthia should kick Daniel out of the house. It's time for tough love or else he'll be sponging off her into his fifties, milking all the perceived grievances of his childhood.

Nan: Cynthia should be in therapy with Daniel because it's helpful to get his viewpoint, but he should *be going to her therapist or at least someone they both see as their therapist.*

Donley: *Daniel has to pay rent and help out around the house, just as one would expect of any adult. The key word here is "expect." Cynthia seems to expect nothing of her son and that's exactly what she's getting.*

Losing a Husband/Losing a Father

by Deborah Levinson

I was widowed at age 44 on Memorial Day. My children were ages 15 and 17. My older son was preparing to go off to college and my younger son was about to get his learner's permit. Everyone was on the move but the dog and me. Sadly, the dog died a short time later. A Hopkins-trained psychotherapist and clinical social worker, my professional skills did not prepare me for this new uncharted world of widowhood and single parenthood into which I had been thrust. Now, a quarter century later, my husband's early death still impact my relationship with my adult children.

Different reactions

Both sons were deeply affected by the loss of their father, but each reacted differently. My older son checked out, while his younger brother appointed himself the "parent child," the one who worked to make sure his family restabilized. Unconsciously, he put his adolescent stage on hold, where it remained until his mid-thirties. At that point he had the time, energy, and focus to deal with his father's death.

My older son stumbled along for years. He connected with a young woman whom he married. In joining closely with his wife's family, he received attention and validation from her father. Sadly, that connection required he give up his own family for all holidays. So my younger son and I were left to figure out holidays for ourselves. My older son found his footing in his career and personal life, especially after he found his calling as a model father. His parenting gave him a deeper sense of self.

One son is still feeling his way

My younger son is currently evolving. Very successful in his first career and sadly unsuccessful in a brief starter marriage (typically entered into by children who lose a parent early), he is exploring new career options and avocational dimensions he did not have the time, energy, or inclination to explore earlier. Still single, he has a wonderful dog, which subsitutes for the passion he had for our family bulldog while he was growing up.

My younger son, my significant other of 22-some-odd years, and my stepdaughter and I celebrate holidays together and have established rituals, such as doing 1000-piece jigsaw puzzles, to foster the bond. We have created our own untraditional family, a blended family, which works for us. My older son will periodically join this group.

Where they are in their own lives

Upon reflection the relationship each of my adult sons has had with me over time seems to have been based on how happy each child has been in his own life at that given moment. While I understood this concept professionally, accepting and living with it emotionally has not always been easy. Importantly, I look for a construct that conceptualizes my relationship with each grown son in a positive way. Thus with my older son we connect frequently about his children, my grandchildren. While I see the children infrequently, they are bonded to me and know "my voice."

After a lot of hard work, patience, and many ups and downs, I am pleased to report that currently I have a good relationship with each of my adult sons and with my stepdaughter. Each relationship is based on the adult child's sphere, not mine. Helping my adult sons deal with an idealized memory of their dead father—and a family that changed way too early for my sons' nascent development—has had many challenges. Yet I kept at it, trying multiple approaches at difficult times. Persistence paid off. Recently my 6-year-old granddaughter, reflecting her father's wistfulness, asked whether I miss my late husband, her deceased grandfather. On the other hand, having finally sold the family home, my younger son noted sweetly, "Mom, home is where you are."

Deborah Levinson, LCSW, published a model on the process of adjustment after major loss and crafting one's next chapter.

Anorexia: The Eating Disorder From Hell

Anorexia nervosa (usually just called anorexia) is characterized by an abnormally low body weight, an intense fear of gaining weight, and a distorted perception of one's body image. Anorexia has the highest death rate of any psychiatric illness, including major depression. The mortality rate associated with the disorder is 12 times higher than the death rate of ALL causes of death for females 15-24 years old, the population most vulnerable to it. Without treatment up to 20 percent of people with serious eating disorders die. Yet many sufferers refuse treatment, at least initially, either because they are in denial or their desire to be thin overrides concerns about their health.

Characteristic behavior

Anorexics may eat tiny amounts of a few "safe" foods, severely restrict their food intake, and/or frequently fast. Some sufferers also exercise excessively. Despite their own spare eating habits, anorexics may prepare elaborate meals for others. They may engage in rigid mealtime rituals, shy away from eating in public, have trouble sleeping and become increasingly irritable. They often try to hide their condition.

According to the Mayo Clinic, the causes of anorexia are complex. As with many diseases, it's most likely a combination of biological, psychological, social, and environmental factors. The Clinic explains that some young people may have a genetic tendency toward perfectionism, sensitivity, and perseverance—all traits associated with anorexia. Some may have obsessive-compulsive personality traits that make it easier to stick to strict diets and forgo food despite being hungry. And they may have high levels of anxiety and engage in restrictive eating to reduce it.

When thinness is glorified

Moreover, modern Western culture emphasizes thinness to an alarming degree. Success and worth are often equated with being thin, and there's enormous peer pressure to look a certain way, particularly among young girls. Finally, people are more vulnerable to anorexia during a transition, such as a new school, home, job or the breakup of a relationship, and while experiencing a loss, especially the death or illness of a loved one.

"Anorexia has nothing to do with food and everything to do with distorted body image," contends therapist Deborah Levinson, LCSW. "And this distorted body image is a metaphor for the young people's feeling about themselves. They feel they are being controlled and by not eating, they're saying, 'You can't make me; I'm the one in control here.'"

Ms. Levinson continues, "Unfortunately, our society equates thinness with beauty, and you're shamed if you can't fit that model. Today, with bullying on social media, the pressures are magnified. Social media is instantaneous, but a young woman can't get thin in an instant and in some cases she can't get thin at all. Often, she shouldn't even be trying."

Distorted body image is at fault

Wendi G. wrote in to say that she used to have her own issues with body image, and she's worried because she's starting to see them in her teenage daughter. In Wendi's case, the anorexia was triggered by a boy telling her no one would date her because she had a big behind. Now she realizes that there were many family dynamics and genetics operating beneath the surface, but at the time she took this boy's cruel remark at face value and began an endless diet. "I never felt thin enough," she said.

Deborah Levinson sees hope. "I have had success by working alongside a nutritionist, who prescribes five small meals a day, and adding structure to the anorexics' lives. I never pressure them to eat. Rather, I concentrate on their strengths and help them feel better about themselves. This positive reinforcement can move mountains."

Losing Zane

by Laura Kenig

L aura Kenig delivered a eulogy at the conclusion of this spring's Speaking of Stories: Personal Stories in Santa Barbara. Laura spoke with great dignity, power, and compassion as she recounted living through a parent's worst nightmare—losing a beloved daughter to anorexia. Here is her script as she wrote it:

> Who's to say how long a person
> Is destined to be here in the physical form?

I had a curly-haired, squeaky-voiced, petite daughter who brought me tremendous joy—from her obsession with the color pink, performing, and ballet to her incredible wit, intelligence, bravery, strength, and sense of humor. She was an artist, and I believe she was her dad's mother reincarnated.

My only child and precious daughter, Zane, was here for 22 years. She died on May 13, 2016 as a result of having been raped when she was 15, leading to a horrific and deadly battle with food. She struggled with anorexia for almost seven years. The last three years of her life she was getting intensive medical help and treatment, which seemed to make her worse—resulting in her becoming actively suicidal.

In the process of watching Zane decline and digesting and absorbing her torment, I came to a place of hopelessness and was eventually able to accept her choice and her right not to have any more medical intervention for her anorexia. There's a lot that led up to me being able to accept her decision.

Mostly the torment

Zane tried to kill herself in October of 2014 and again in October of 2015 and ended up in the hospital both times. It's a long and complex story, and she might still be alive today if she had not been raped. But I also believe that the medical model of intervention for her eating disorder was a form of rape of her soul. After her second suicide attempt in October of 2015, Zane made a valiant effort to get her life back. She got out of the medical model of treatment, but she was not able to overcome the eating disorder and ultimately decided she would rather die from it than go back into treatment. I honored her wishes.

When she announced that she would no longer drink water a few days after her 22nd birthday in April of 2016, I knew that she was choosing to die and I spent the next month by her side. With the support of my husband and hospice, I watched my daughter die.

Six months prior to Zane's death, in November of 2015, she wrote the following letter to my parents:

"My mom asked me to write my thoughts on where I am at with my situation so that she will be able to talk to you about me and her reactions to my decisions.

Here goes. . . .

As you both know, it has been a pretty rough few years for me, most of which have been spent inside institutions of one sort or another. Predominantly, these places have focused on my anorexia, restoring my weight, administering medications, and attempting to provide therapy. Unfortunately, most of the places I have gone to have been remarkably close-minded in their approach to healing, focusing on labeling me and not acknowledging what I have to offer the world. While my time in treatment has often saved my physical life, it is clear to me that it has killed off all other aspects of who I am. My spirit has been shattered, along with my mental capacity and will to exist.

I succumbed to the world of modern medicine, a world of fear and us-against them conversations, where the patient is treated as less intelligent or capable than the so-called professionals. I know that all of these people had good intentions in their attempts to help me. They were never malicious, but it seems to me that they were misdirected. It is for that reason that I have decided to never return to an institution to seek help for myself, especially if that institution specializes in eating disorders.

I say all of this because I am at a point with my weight and eating where I ordinarily would be placed back in treatment, but I have chosen to put my foot down and say no to this form of supposed healing. I made a lot of progress—working with my new therapists—Terri and Becky. They approach me with love and compassion as well as respect and have helped me to bring my ailing spirit, mind, and will slowly back to life. I feel more alive now than I have in recent years.

I am asking myself and those around me tricky philosophical questions about life, death, and everything in between. I am exploring yoga, hiking, contra dancing, making friends out the world of treatment, listening to my dad's music, and am going to school again. All of this is to say that I am unwilling to let these aspects of me die in order to save my body.

I am willing to die in the physical sense, if that is in fact what happens—in order to not lose the sense of voice and self that I have re-gained. This is radical, even dangerous. It can appear preposterous to someone on the outside. After all, I am a 21-year-old with the potential to do many great things. As I am often reminded. But, those great things will never happen if I am continually being kept alive in an institution of some sort. Perhaps I will, with more time outside the medical world, have a shift in willingness and begin to eat sustainably. Wouldn't that be nice? I hope it happens, but speaking realistically I am likely to die from anorexia. But I will die in my full power, living a life I have chosen, experiencing what it is like to be me.

If you have any questions, or want to talk more about any or all of this, please feel free to email back. I know my mom will want to talk to you both about this, as she asked me to send this to you in order to be able to do so. It is a really horrifying place to be in as a parent—a place I can only imagine as I have never had a child. I am lucky to have open-minded, loving parents as well as grandparents like you two.

My best to you and much love,

Zane

A mother's letter

Just prior to Zane's death, I wrote the following letter to friends and family:

Our dearest daughter, Zane, is going to be free from her suffering soon and is getting closer by the day.

Phone calls with family and friends, advisors and teachers—saying goodbye.

She is running out of steam.

Speaking in whispers.

Zayde, her beloved Grandfather, and friend Judy are her constant companions waiting for her to join them on the other side.

Her strong, athletic body has withstood so much and is determined to keep her going in spite of her emaciated and anorexic condition.

This process is slow and agonizing.

It's also filled with beauty.

The beauty of slowing down and just being together.

Carrying her outside today for some fresh air.

The lilac ritual.

The gift of listening so intently it hurts. And hurts.

The gift of tears.

Zane reaching for me in the middle of the night.

Sleeping in the hospital bed with my precious daughter.

The gift of memories.

Loving her.

Massaging her.

Luxuriating baths and hair washes.

I'm so grateful for this time together!

Singing to her – Special songs

Hebrew songs.

Prascilla Ahn's song, 'Dream' (listen to it if you can)

Sara Thomsen's songs, 'Holy Angels' and 'The Beauty of the Dancer'

Deva Premal and the Gayatri Mantra

Alyssa's song, 'I Love Your So Much,' and her devoted friendship

Encircling Zane with our love.

The gift of hospice and AWESOME nurse Jennifer.

Giving Zane meds—trying to stay ahead of her physical pain and anxiety.

Buying a baby monitor to hear her if we aren't in the room.

Splitting the night shift with her dad. He the first half, me the second.

Zane wanting us to be together for meals.

Hers: 'Charms' Sweet 'n Sour suckers.

Today the blue tongue — 'Sweet Blue Raspberry' flavor.

"I wish we were home in Minnesota. I'd like us all to take our clothes off and jump into a cool lake," said Zane.

Laughing together.

Crying together.

Anger.

Frustration.

Grief.

The insanity of this eating disorder—insisting on daily weigh-ins—the torment continues.

"We would not be in this situation if it weren't for this eating disorder," says Zane.

End stage of a deadly and chronic disease.

No more medical interventions leading to walled-in, institutional settings not recognizing the beauty and individuality and needs of our precious daughter.

I love her so much I am letting her go.

IT'S THE RIGHT THING TO DO.

I know her agony, as a mother knows her daughter's agony.

No one should have to bear what she has borne.

I suppose you could say that about me as her mother and about my mother as mother and grandmother.

I know my mother feels this agony.

My heart goes out to her.

And Joey, Zane's dad.
We have been so blessed by this precious being in our lives.
She is so worthy.
Worthy of freedom from torment.
Worthy of all the love that is flowing her way.
My heart is filled with gratitude to have known this dear,
sweet soul—
My teacher of kindness and grace.
My little elephant.
Boombaji.
Sweet pea.
Little bird.
Little bear.
My heart.

Readers' Comments

A mother's love is beyond understanding, I've always said to my children there is nothing I wouldn't do for you because I love you so much. This mother and father did the ultimate thing in allowing their daughter to be who she needed to be. Such bravery, such love. Thank you for your gift. N.C.

Laura, Joey, and Zane have given their friends a lesson in love that is tender and terrible. That Laura is sharing with others is such a gift, for it may provide understanding and comfort to those who also struggle with keeping the spirit alive at the expense of the body. Laura and Joey's courage to share their experience honors Zane's life. J.R.

Chapter 8

Leaving a Legacy

At some point you will probably start thinking about leaving a legacy for your children and grandchildren. First, though, you have to deal with legal documents, such as estate plans and instructions on how you want to be treated at the end of your life. Then there are the discussions with family about their inheritance and your final wishes, neither of which are easy conversations. Here, you'll get advice from experts to help you take care of the mechanics as properly and painlessly as possible.

Going from these serious topics to a lighter, although no less consuming subject, you might want to tackle the issue of downsizing. Once upon a time, you could have simply left everything to your adult children. Now, as they are both less sentimental and more space-constrained than you, they probably don't want your "stuff." Even the Salvation Army is balking at taking unsalable items these days! I pass along the organizers' do's and don'ts for downsizing (although some of you told me you're secretly hoping gracious living will make a comeback and your kids will take everything).

Finally, beyond your material goods, you want to leave your adult children a legacy of your values, achievements, and character. You might be asking yourself what you want them to remember *about* you and what they should carry forward *from* you? These final articles are designed to give you some good ideas.

Shadow Box of the Heart

by Linda Schwartz

I put the finishing touches on the shadow box
close the lid of the assembled memorabilia
of my mother's life

her thick gold-rimmed bifocals
  a miniature suitcase symbolic of her love of travel
    Mah Jongg tiles embellished with intricate designs
      her scuffed   well-used Nordstrom charge card
        a sterling silver sewing thimble
          playing cards and plastic poker chips
            her wedding invitation tinged yellow with age
              black and white photos of her as a young bride

nestled on a pristine-white satin backdrop
these mementos are a mere glimpse
of wife   mother   sister
grandmother   great-grandmother   friend

missing behind the wooden frame
the essence of who she was
too elusive and ephemeral
to be pinned onto satin
instead held steadfast
in the shadow box
of my heart

Linda Schwartz is the author of Reflections: Poems about Life,
Relationships, and Family.

Last Wishes, Part 1: The Conversation

If there's one thing your grown children don't want to hear about, it's a world without you. "Oh, Mother, you're so morbid!" they'll say when a parent tries to broach the subject. They'll clamp their hands over their ears, chant a nursery rhyme, or even run from the room—anything rather than confront the issue of their parent's mortality. Susan Plummer, PhD, Executive Director of the Alliance for Living and Dying Well, urges you to persevere.

"To get 'the Conversation' started, you can thank your children for giving you the gift of peace of mind by allowing you to communicate how you want to be treated at the end of your life, says Plummer. "There is a real comfort for you in their knowing your choices, thereby maximizing the chance that those choices will be respected.

It's adult to prepare

"You are also giving them a real gift. You are modeling adult responsibility in the form of preparation. Moreover, you are revealing yourself as a nuanced individual, not just a cardboard cutout of a parent. And it shows you see a role for them in your well-being. Your relationship can become more intimate and compassionate as result.

"It's more effective if the whole family is there at the same time for 'the Conversation.' Then everyone hears the same thing at the same time. If your child is married, it is better if his/her spouse is in the room; the more ears on the topic, the better. Someone could take notes and distribute it to all members of the family afterward. For those families whose members who are scattered, there's always Skype, FaceTime, etc. One family I know of even had the Conversation at Thanksgiving, when the matriarch put her wishes in the form of an advance care directive on each plate and said, 'We're not going to eat until we go over mine and you fill out yours!'

"If, despite all your efforts, you are still meeting resistance from your adult children, you might try a third-party facilitator. Some retirement homes, churches and community centers have parent/child advance planning workshops, which helps to depersonalize the subject. However you do it, realize that the Conversation is not just for old people and it shouldn't take place just once. The more you have it, the more routine and matter-of-fact it becomes. It's like lab work, just another part of high-quality health care."

Last Wishes, Part 2: The Document

In previous article, I discussed 'the Conversation' in which you share your end-of-life wishes with your grown offspring. Now, I will turn my attention to the document, called an Advance Care Directive (ACD), that makes your wishes legal. While most of us think of the ACD as a conveyance for our basic desires, such as "Do not resuscitate," nowadays the document can be much more detailed, down to even the kind music you want to hear at the end! The ACD speaks for you when you cannot speak for yourself.

Important for you and your children

Creating an Advance Care Directive is as important for your adult children as it is for you. At the time of a medical crisis there's great confusion and grief. Families may argue about treatment, physicians may become demoralized by competing instructions, and the patient's wishes my get lost in the shuffle. Moreover, without a blueprint to follow, after-grief may be complicated by regret. According to Dr. Susan Plummer, Executive Director of the Alliance for Living and Dying Well, there is evidence-based research that a month after a family member's passing, those who had an Advance Care Directive to work with showed less anxiety, depression, and post-traumatic stress syndrome than those who didn't.

Bear in mind that an ACD is not just for old people. Anyone over 18 should have one because when head injuries occur—and, let's face it, accidents do happen to young people, too—they may not be able to communicate their wishes. Encourage your children, especially if they have children of their own, to fill out the form. It will force them to consider such key issues as guardianship and financial support until their children come of age. In fact, you can offer to fill out your ACD's together.

Distribute copies

Once you've completed the document, keep the original with your other estate planning papers. Make copies for your adult children and whomever else will be involved, including your physician and your local hospital or clinic, where it should become part of your chart.

There are different versions of the Advance Care Directive. Some forms are legal in some states and some in others, but even if you type out your wishes on a plain piece of paper, sign it, and have it notarized, the paper is legal. The Alliance for Living and Dying Well favors the Five Wishes, which has been used by more than 25 million people and is available online for a small fee at *www.agingwithdignity.org*. Says Susan Plummer, "There are many scenarios, not all of which you can anticipate, but if your offspring and physician get the gist of your end-of-life wishes, they are more likely to carry them out."

Controlling or Conceding?

Bob and Lynda Cronyn give their single-mom daughter, Shira, $1,000 a month. *Their gift is intended to let Shira only work part-time so she can be with her son more fully. This year Shira wants to spend most of that money on a fancy sleep-away camp for him, which the Cronyns feel is a frivolous use of the money. What should they do?*

- *Speak up?*
- *Withhold the allowance because Shira seems to be frittering it away?*
- *Go along with their daughter?*

The Panel Weighs In:

Richard: *The Cronyn's have forfeited their right to speak up. The word "gift" implies no strings attached. Also, the camp may be such a valuable experience for the kid that it's worth every penny.*

Janine: *They have to go along with Shira even if they don't agree with her. Otherwise, they're using their money to manipulate her.*

Hank: *With hindsight the Cronyns probably should have stipulated how they wanted the money to be used, for example, only for educational purposes. Now Shira is counting on their commitment. They could voice their concerns, however.*

Beth: *The Cronyns should just keep doing what they're doing. Since they didn't specify the use of the allowance, they have to comply with Shira's wishes.*

Why *Not* to Name Your Child As Executor

In the past people automatically named an adult child, close friend or financial institution as executor of their estate. But today there's another option: the private professional fiduciary. A relatively new phenomenon, the professional fiduciary takes the burden off loved ones at a difficult time and, frankly, does a better job of it.

Not for the faint-hearted—or the amateur—settling an estate often entails a myriad of tasks: identifying and collecting all of the estate's assets, depositing those funds into the estate bank account; settling all debts; preparing and filing a final tax return; having real estate appraised and readied for sale; seeing that all other possessions are identified and valuated—the list goes on and on. Moreover, if a living trust has not been set up, the will must be probated through the courts. Needless to say, the job of executor can be overwhelming.

Dealing with several agencies

It can also take a long time. The executor might have to deal with the IRS, DMV, County agencies, and various financial institutions, some of which are more cooperative than others. I personally remember going back and forth with the IRS for months over a disputed $1.99 item in my mother's estate! The professional fiduciary has the know-how and contacts in the community to make the process go more quickly. If an heir can only get to these matters at nights and on weekends and/or lives out of town, things can drag on even longer. According to Courtney

DeSoto, principal at Channel Islands Fiduciary Group, "Beneficiaries can be very unrealistic. They think they will get their distribution in six months, but one to two years is the more likely time frame."

Addressing their concerns

Even more onerous than dealing with logistics is dealing with squabbling heirs. The private professional fiduciary acts as an impartial liaison, whose experience in these matters enables her to come up workable solutions that are fair to everyone. Without such a referee in a position of authority, one sibling might pressure another to sell a beloved vacation home, resentments among first and second families might surface, and even families that once got along famously might suddenly stop speaking to one another. Although an inheritance represents found money, the literature suggests that families can go to war over the most inconsequential things.

Even if they know all that, adult children are often offended and suspicious when they learn that their parents have named a private professional fiduciary in their wills, not knowing, among other things, that fiduciaries are paid out of the estate. To address their concerns you might want to call a getting-to-know-you meeting. Here, the fiduciary can explain how she provides a great deal of safety and security for the assets.

In California, for example, the Professional Fiduciaries Bureau ensures that professional fiduciaries have undergone a criminal background check and are insured, bonded, and up-to-date on the latest rules and regulations regarding trusts and estates. Moreover, they must have passed a licensing exam and continue to take education courses in their field.

The private professional fiduciary is not the children's adversary. To the contrary, "My responsibility is to the beneficiaries," says DeSoto. "I want to do what is best for them. While I can't always make everyone happy, I can at least make them comfortable with the process. Using a licensed, neutral third-party provides that the matter is handled with the highest legal and ethical standards. Communications and transparency are a must. I've found that when everything is explained to the children, they're actually relieved that the estate is in a professional's hands so they don't have to deal with it."

The Smart Way to Give Money

While many parents are of a mind to give their grown kids money today as opposed to leaving it to them as an inheritance in the future, many experts caution that by making such financial gifts they run the risk of encouraging a cycle of dependency that's hard to break. Indeed, many POGOs have told me they are still giving handouts to, if not wholly supporting, "kids" in their thirties, forties, and beyond. The experts say that even if you can afford these gifts, by making them you may be sapping your offspring's motivation to work hard and succeed financially, which is the opposite of their intended purpose. In other words, there's no such thing as a free lunch—either for your adult children or for you.

According to Nashville financial adviser Trey Smith, "Regular checks engender regular expectations. If you write your kids a check annually three consecutive years, your generosity may become habit-forming for them." In thinking about this issue, Smith has devised what he calls the Rule of Three: "The first check is greatly appreciated, the second one is appreciated, but less of a surprise and the third is still appreciated, but no surprise at all. After the third time, they may come to expect a check every year."

Smith has also come up with three strategies for making financial presents to your adult children:

1. Keep it irregular. Vary the time of year you send checks and don't send them every year. While dependency stems from expectation, breaking things up creates doubt—and independance.

2. Don't always give money directly. There are various ways to assist your grown kids indirectly. These include paying their uninsured medical expenses, helping out with a purchase by a grandchild (such as a first car), providing cash for a home remodeling project and covering some expenses for a first baby (such as a stroller, a car seat, a crib or a year's supply of diapers). Varying the circumstances of your assistance tends to make gifts unexpected and appreciated windfalls, instead of something recipients come to count on.

3. Confine your help to rare occasions. For example, expenses for key anniversaries or birthdays could qualify. After all, how often does your daughter have a 20th wedding anniversary or her son have a 16th birthday? Another irregular impetus would be the need for plane fare and lodging to attend family reunions, assuming these events aren't annual or bi-annual. And then there are the occasional family vacations for the extended family.

Whether you can give the money without tax consequences to the recipient is beside the point, in the experts' opinion, as is the desire to reduce the size of one's estate to mitigate inheritance taxes. Even if you were rolling in dough, they would tell you to keep your assistance unpredictable. By doing so you will be doing your children the great favor of helping them become more self-reliant.

How to Talk With Your Adult Kids About Their Inheritance

by Lori R. Sackler

W hat's the best way to tell our grown children about our estate plans without creating a family drama?" That's the question I'm most often asked when I tell people I've written a new book about money, family and communications, *The M Word: The Money Talk Every Family Needs to Have About Wealth and Their Financial Future.* It's no wonder: More than $15 trillion will be transferred to the next generation between 2007 and 2026.

Most family transfers are flawed

Problem is, there's a 70 percent failure rate when transferring family wealth from one generation to another —a loss of control of assets through mismanagement, poor investments or the like, according to Roy Williams and Vic Preisser, two of the founders of the Institute for Preparing Heirs. Many of these failures occur because families don't do enough to prepare their heirs for the handoff. It's like giving your 16-year-old son the keys to your car without a driving lesson. Being unprepared to inherit money won't kill someone, of course, but it can certainly wreak emotional, mental, and financial destruction.

The conversations parents don't have

Unfortunately, most parents fuel rather than prevent this kind of havoc. They think: "I'd rather not talk about it" or "We'll set up a time to chat about it later." The "it" in these phrases is, of course, money. In far too many families, money is a dirty word, a taboo subject, what I call the M word. But in my experience, one of the most common conflicts among family members arises when they are probating an estate that hasn't been previously discussed. Regardless of whether all the children will get exactly the same inheritance, if they know in advance what the will says, the parents can reduce anxiety in an already stressful situation. Generally speaking, what you should tell your adult children about your estate ought to be guided by your family's values and by each child's ability to handle the information.

When one child has special circumstances

In many families with grown kids, there is one child who has issues involving money. This could be the result of his or her bad habits or perhaps a physical, mental or emotional challenge. In that case, you might need to have a separate conversation with him or her and create a special arrangement that will work for these circumstances. Otherwise, though, I think a balanced approach to sharing information about family wealth is the best option.

Who'll get the jewelry?

It's extremely important to have a conversation with your adult children about who will get your personal property. That's because one of the most contentious aspects of settling an estate can be the distribution of things like Mom's diamond engagement ring, Dad's collection of abstract expressionist artwork or Great-Grandma's gold-plated china. This is just as true for items that aren't worth much money but have a great deal of sentimental value.

When you have this conversation, give each child a chance to talk about his or her favorite items and come to an agreement about how everything will be divided up. Not only will this give your family members a chance to share stories and talk openly about items that mean a lot to them, it will encourage a healthy dialogue and cooperative spirit regarding estate matters. This will prove to be extremely valuable down the road.

The family estate planning meeting

After the discussion about personal property, you may want to have an attorney draft a simple summary of your estate plans and distribute it to your heirs. Then, hold a family meeting to review the document and answer any questions. Before I talk about that meeting, a word of advice: As a rule, when it comes to family wealth, I've found it best to treat your children equally in your will. Of course, if one is incapacitated in some way or has special needs, like autism, you may want to provide additional financial assistance through a special needs trust, an insurance policy or a larger portion of the estate.

That brings me back to the family meeting about your estate plans. In this session, which should happen well in advance of any wealth transfer, you'll want to tell your grown kids where your important financial documents are located, what they can expect in the will, and what roles they may play in the future managing the estate. If one child will get a bigger inheritance than the others for reasons like the ones I noted earlier, this is the time to say so. Otherwise, if the kids find out when the will is read, you might unleash a tsunami of emotions, which could have largely been avoided through advance conversations.

By explaining to all your kids why one child will be given a larger share and writing a will that says, in effect, "I love you all just as much, but this is what we felt we had to do as parents," you may avoid bad feelings and the possibility of a contested will.

How to make the meeting successful

Before the talk, determine the goals and objectives you want to achieve and draft an outline or an agenda, with a few talking points. Choose a quiet place for the meeting that will make everyone feel comfortable and secure. During the session, speak in a calming tone and use such words words as "safety," "security" and "protection."

If the environment gets toxic, don't lash out or shut down out of fear, anger, embarrassment, defensiveness or any other unpleasant feeling. Make sure everyone has an opportunity to speak. Should thorny issues arise, try to come up with solutions. It can be helpful to have a trusted adviser—like your accountant, attorney or financial planner—at this family meeting, to help ensure an atmosphere of tolerance, patience and impartiality.

But no matter how skilled a pro you invite, remember that you're the one ultimately responsible for ensuring a successful transfer of your estate.

This article by financial adviser Lori R. Sackler originally appeared on the website Next Avenue, www.nextavenue.org.

It's Come to This

Cynthia is making out a new will, and she's wondering whether to put her eldest child, Susan, in it. She and Susan have been estranged for years, to the point where Susan will not even let her attend her own grandchildren's high school graduations. What should Cynthia do?

- Is she obligated to treat Susan the same as her other offspring in the will?
- Should she leave a lesser amount to Susan?
- Is Cynthia justified in cutting her out altogether?
- And, if so, should she include a letter in the will explaining her actions?

The Panel Weighs In:

Justin: Since Susan has chosen to excise Cynthia from her life, Cynthia should just leave her daughter a token amount in her will and leave the rest of her portion to Susan's children.

Glenny: I disagree. I think you have to leave equal amounts to all your children no matter what. Until the day she died, my mother cried over being cut out of her father's will. Besides, you don't want to create conflict among the children over their inheritance.

Alex: I think the litmus test should be who needs the money most not how they treated you. If one child is successful and one is not, why not help out where you could do the most good?

Marie: Speaking of doing the most good, I think

Cynthia should leave Susan's portion to charity. If Susan didn't want her mother in her life while she was alive, why should Cynthia show up in her life after she's dead?

Reader's Comment

If the child has completely abandoned the parent, then , no, after a certain time, she should not be remembered in the will. The other children will certainly understand and may even resent it if she is, in fact, included. I agree with equal amounts to all that are still involved in the family rather than by need, because all would hope they had been loved equally. H.S.

The Downsizing Dilemma, Part I: The Kids Don't Want The China

Many parents whose kids have flown the nest are thinking of downsizing. Moving to smaller quarters means making a million decisions, not the least of which is what to save *for* the children and what to save the children from.

In *"Sorry, Nobody Wants Your Parents' Stuff,"* which he wrote for *www.nextavenue.com*, Richard Eisenberg quotes Mary Kay Buysse, executive director of the National Association of Senior Move Managers, "This is an Ikea and Target generation. They live minimally, much more so than the boomers. They don't have the emotional connection to things that earlier generations did. And they're more mobile. So they don't want a lot of heavy stuff dragging down a move across the country for a new opportunity."

It's hard not to feel rejected

If you offer your treasured possessions to your children and they don't want them, it's hard not to take it as a rejection of you, your values, and your lifestyle. But, honestly, while your grown offspring are fighting for every inch of living space, why should they get dewy-eyed over Grandma Edie's iced tea spoons?

If you daughter hasn't unpacked her wedding dishes after six years, what makes you think she'll want yours? If your son eats on paper plates and uses plastic forks, why would he get excited about Wedgewood service for 12, even if it has been in your family for generations. Let's get real about the silver that needs polishing, the hand-painted china that can't go in the dishwasher, and the gold-rimmed cups that blow up in the microwave. Apparently, even the Salvation Army is steering away from such impractical relics of "gracious living."

In addition to wanting to preserve your family's heritage by giving your heirlooms to your children, you may feel you're providing them with items of great value. Alas, that's generally not the case due to changing tastes. According to Roger Schrenk and Chris Fultz, who own Nova Liquidation and also wrote for nextavenue, "Sadly, the value of handmade antiques has been dropping since Nancy Reagan was in the White House... in many cases you can now easily spend more on 10 dining chairs from Restoration Hardware than for 10 made in the 1920s."

Not worth what you think

It's also matter of supply and demand. Schrenk and Fultz say that "brown furniture," which was mass produced quickly after WWII is worth very little today. Ditto silver plate, which probably includes most of the chafing dishes, trays, flatware, and candlesticks you've inherited or bought. They're most likely made of copper or brass with a micro-thin layer of silver on the top.

Even full sets of sterling silver aren't what they used to be. According to Schrenk and Fultz, "Since the crash of 2008, most sterling silver flatware sets have become uncollectible." As for rugs, they contend, "Unless you've got truly antique, vegetable-dyed rugs with an unbelievably dense knot count, you will be lucky to get 10 percent of the purchase price."

What to save

So, what's a downsizing parent to do? Some experts say to dispose of everything, letting the children pick what they love and can use now. Others recommend putting together a small box of objects from their childhood that will have sentimental value. But all say your grown offspring will thank you profusely for saving them from having to dispose of your possessions themselves. Of course, if you are also storing their possessions, that's another story for another day.

The Downsizing Dilemma, Part 2: What Stays and What Goes?

In "The Downsizing Dilemma, Part 1," we saw that our kids don't want our stuff. That's the *why* of getting rid of things. But even after we POGOs have accepted this painful truth, we're still left with the *how* of it. All those decisions! All those fond memories! All those irrational attachments! Here's what the experts advise:

Don't even think about renting a storage unit

You're just postponing the inevitable. Americans can rationalize keeping anything and apparently we do. In 1995 just one in 17 households rented a unit; now it's one in 10. No wonder there are almost 50,000 self-storage facilities in this country, double the number of McDonald's and Starbucks locations combined. Moreover, we shell out big bucks for these units; on average the popular 10' × 10' storage pod costs nearly $2,000 a year. According to Ann Gambrell, a professional organizer, "People end up spending money because they can't make a decision." If that sounds familiar, ask yourself:

Do I have to go it alone? A disinterested party (obviously not your spouse) can act as the voice of reason. Bribe a friend, bring in someone who arranges yard sales, or engage a certified appraiser. Also, think about hiring a teen to put all your loose photos into albums and/or do the heavy lifting.

Could I get another one easily? We all keep so many

things because "We might need it someday." But even if you ever do need it, which is doubtful, could you get it easily? Downsizer Smallin Kuper applies a 20/20 rule. "If you have a used possession that you could repurchase for $20 or less or borrow from a neighbor in 20 minutes or less, toss it," she says.

How many do I really need? If you were living on a boat, would you use more than one cutting board, one sauté pan, and one comfy reading chair? Keep that nautical image in mind. The same applies to collections, where one fine cup could represent the whole of your mother's old tea set, for example. If you photograph the rest, parting with it will be much easier.

Have I got room for it? Most of us vastly overestimate the capacity of our new, downsized space. One woman told me she was getting nowhere discarding furniture because every time she and her husband considered one of their pieces, he said breezily, "Oh, that will to into my new study." "Right," she thought to herself, "if it were the size of Versailles." She finally had to bring in a space planner to bring her husband down to earth.

Could I resell or get a tax deduction for the castoffs? If the answer is yes, you might get a lot more excited about selling and donating. Many people do well on Craigslist, eBay, and other online resale sites, especially if they do their homework on how comparable items are priced. Other people use Close5 and letgo, apps that connect buyers and sellers who live near one another. And still others are comfortable with no-tech solutions, such as yard and estate sales. Giving away has its advantages, too. Tax deductions can become meaningful if you donate a substantial amount of goods to charitable organizations. The psychic rewards can be even more meaningful, because you're helping the less fortunate today while saving your kids from the pain of sorting through your things tomorrow.

Nostalgia is not your friend

Many of us could part with a ratty old sofa without too much angst, and books and clothing aren't too emotionally loaded, either, says organizing guru Marie Kondo. But if you start reading just one old love letter, you'll be lost on Memory Lane for hours. The same goes for photo albums. The solution to the latter is digitizing—which guarantees you'll never look at those photos again.

Not so susceptible to digitizing are old scrapbooks. If you can't part with the swizzle sticks from your senior prom or the cocktail napkins that say "Dawn's Sweet 16," don't. Set aside these personal treasures in a half-way space. When you come back to them and they still, in Kondo's phrase, "spark joy," I say keep 'em, even if the only place they can go is the sock drawer.

Downsizers will tell you that when you divest yourself of possessions, you feel liberated and free to focus on what's really important, like your grown kids. But, hey, wasn't your son supposed to retrieve that 15-year-old rusty bike he's so sentimental about? And wasn't your daughter going to take back the moldy cheerleader outfit she swears represents the apex of her life? They better hurry up; curbside pickup is only three days away. . . .

A Serious Medical Situation

Kathy, who is divorced and lives alone, was just told that she has an aggressive form of breast cancer that requires a radical mastectomy with follow-up chemotherapy. Although she longs to have her daughter, Maureen, by her side throughout the ordeal, she's loath to ask for her help or even tell her about the diagnosis. Maureen has two young children plus a demanding job and lives 250 miles away.

- Should Kathy not tell Maureen until after the operation?
- Ask Maureen to come down for the operation?
- Rely on her friends instead of her daughter?

The Panel Weighs In:

Vicki: I think Kathy should lay out the situation for Maureen and let her daughter come up with a solution that would work for both of them.

Alyssa: Kathy should work out a "caring tree" among her friends so she'll have support throughout the postoperative period. Maureen is just a lucky extra, given how far away she lives and all her obligations.

Gary: If not now, when? This is what adult families do when the chips are down.

Mario: Maureen would never forgive herself—or her mother—if she were not included in this family crisis.

What Do You Owe Your Adult Children?

As a historian of childhood, I've long wondered what purpose the family serves once the children leave home. After all, we no longer live under one roof, till the fields side-by-side or even mind the store together. Still, there seems to be a residual sense of obligation on both sides, even if there's no consensus as to what that looks like. When I asked a number of parents what they thought they owed their adult children, their answers ranged from "24/7 support' to "zilch." Here are some representative comments:

Parents feel they owe their kids financial support

"Because my daughter got into a prestigious private college, I remortgaged my house to help pay the $250,000 bill. She can't get a full-time job, so I'm still helping her out."

"I am able to afford it, so I help out with private schools, camps, and extracurricular activities for the grandchildren. It makes me feel good to know that I'm making an impact on their lives. I also consider it an investment in their futures."

"My kids are self-sufficient and never ask us for anything."

"After the kids are a certain age, everything a parent gives is discretionary. There are no 'shoulds.' And if you give more to one child than another because he has fewer resources, so be it. You can't make everyone happy."

Parents feel the need to show up

"My son and his wife work hard so I'm happy to make dinner for them once a week at their home and babysit."

"I fly across the country every six weeks to be in my grandchildren's lives."

"My daughter finagled her husband to move across the country, leaving his own close family behind, so she could be closer to us when we become infirm. Until then I will do whatever I can do physically for her and her family because I see her commitment to me."

"I moved several states away just to be near my daughter."

"If my kids needed me or my husband for emergency. I would gladly give up my activities for them."

"I went to every recital, soccer match, and school play when my kids were little. I'm doing the same for my grandchildren."

Parents want to be emotionally supportive

"I think it's important to share my wisdom (even if I'm not asked for it very often) so that my children hear a viewpoint different from their own."

"I know my son doesn't see it, but I feel I owe him the security of knowing that I will always be there for him."

"My two thirty-something daughters are my right and left arms; I'd do anything for them. This might be unhealthy *and naïve, but I don't understand boundaries where they are concerned."*

"Like a precious friend, I want to do whatever I can do to boost and empower my kids."

"I want to be available."

"I owe it to them to show an interest in their lives."

"I'm trying not to make life hard for them."

"I owe it to my children to be a role model and make them proud of me for being a hard worker and community volunteer."

Parents don't want to be an encumbrance

"I don't want to be a barnacle clinging for dear life to their raft."

"I don't want to be a burden to them."

"When I get old I don't expect them to change my diapers."

"Their wives probably wouldn't want to take me in, but since my sons are responsible human beings, they would make arrangements for my care."

Looking back, looking ahead

"I want to leave my daughter a legacy of pretty things, like china, paintings and my best household goods. My mother walked out on our family when I was eight and left me nothing."

"After I'm gone I feel I owe my son a financial inheritance, which will be the proceeds from my house."

"I owe my twenty-something daughters nothing. My job as a parent is done. I could move halfway around the world and they would be fine. I enjoy them, I send them love and emotional support, but I feel that when college is over they are on their own. I will divide my assets 50-50 upon my death—which reminds me, I really need to make out a will!"

When to Stop Subsidizing Adult Children?

F rank continued giving his son, Dirk, an allowance even
after Dirk got his first job. After all, Frank rationalized,
on his small starting salary, there was no way Dirk could
cover his student loans, car payments and rent and still
have any kind of life. But that was almost a decade ago
and Frank has yet to pull the plug because some sort of
financial emergency always seems to bedevil Dirk. What
should Frank do?

- Have a candid discussion with Dirk about the
  young man's standing on his own two feet and then
  withdrawing the subsidy?

- Taper off?

- Continue to help out because the cost of housing and
  everything else is so high today?

The Panel Weighs In:

Suzette: Frank should set a date three months hence
and let his son know that the party's over.

Pete: I agree. After ten years on his own, Dirk should
be able to live within his means or get into another line
of work.

Ilana: I like the tapering off approach. Then the father
doesn't come across as the heavy, and the pain is not as
acute as it would be with a guillotine chop.

Rich: Dirk has probably been expecting his father to

cut off the allowance for years. Frank may be surprised that his son is not surprised by his announcement!

Readers' Comments

I had this problem with both my children and in preparation for retirement, I had a chat with both and told them the Bank of Mom is now closed, out of business, and from now on, I will no longer be able to supplement their incomes. So, when they get a traffic ticket, have gotten in trouble and need an attorney, or have a house issue, they will need to have a savings account for emergency needs; it will no longer come from me. This gave them a heads up so they could prepare. They tested me a few times and were met with, "I don't have the extra cash because I am going to be retiring soon." M.H.

Wow! You are my hero and I bet you are your children's hero, too. Guilt, resentment, and enabling not spoken here. S.S.

Enabling to the max. How old is Sam? 18 or 40? At 18 some guidance and monitoring might be helpful, but at 40? Let Sam feel the consequences of his own behavior. G.F.

"Consequences of his own behavior" is a great concept, but a hard one for enabling parents who are "just trying to help." W. C.

What's In Your Memory Box?

Just because our kids don't want our china and silverware, that doesn't mean they don't want to know more about us. When I asked several POGO readers what they would put in a memory box for their grown offspring and grandchildren, here's what they replied:

Carol Brumberger: Pictures and names of our parents and grandparents.

Rita Gershengorn: Recordings of all the original songs I've written through the years, including songs I wrote for their Bar and Bat Mitzvah and their weddings, plus all kinds of photographs, a video of a show I was in, and videos of shows I wrote and directed for children.

Susan Lang: I would include cards and letters of appreciation that I have received [as a teacher and therapist]. I would also include special cards or notes my children or grandchildren had written. After my mom passed away, I found a box of a few notes I had written to my parents at important times in my life. I was touched to see that they had been saved and was surprised at what I had written!

Jon Greenleaf: Baseball glove and baseball, Mets hat, a copy of McCullough's "Truman," photo of you and me together, photo of dollhouse recipient with house, one of my photographs, recording of Liszt's "Les Preludes" and Tchaikovsky's "Romeo and Juliet," photo of my parents, recording of Louis Armstrong's Dixieland band playing "When the Saints Go Marching In," recording of the Cornell alma mater, photo of 1955 Brooklyn Dodger World Series champions, photo of us with children, photo of us with grandchildren, your engagement photo.

Deb Levinson: Book on warm fuzzies and cold pricklies.

Susette Naylor: My father's autobiography—because it explains all the formative aspects of my young life and the aspects that I continually struggle to integrate with being bi-cultural and marrying into this culture. Photos of me within my birth family—because they have been and will be a part of the next generations' lives. Our wedding certificate in Chinese—as performed by the Consul General—and a wedding photograph. A letter from me. Photo of me at Museum of Natural History in New York in the China Exhibit I helped with. Photo of me in Namibia at a construction site and one here [as an architect]. Copies of the curriculum I put together when I was Director of the Bay Area China Education Project at Stanford/Berkeley as a graduate student. Three Chinese items—2 calligraphic and 1 chop for my daughter: One with our family poem, one with something my dad had done when I graduated from Vassar, and my chop that my father carved with the old characters. Ack, that's a ridiculously large box!

Donne Davis: I have 3 items I would put in a memory box for my children and grandchildren. They each represent a different creative project my husband, Sonny, and I collaborated on:

Dreyer's Official Ice Cream Taster Scrapbook. Sonny nominated Donne to be a taster, and she was one of ten chosen out of 10,000 entries. She won a two-night stay at a hotel in Berkeley, CA, and a day at the Dreyer's plant sampling new ice cream flavors.

Invitation to Donne and Sonny's 25th Wedding Anniversary. The Davises wrote the words for the vows' renewal ceremony, which their thirty guests found very moving.

Off Center—A Collection of Cartoons by Sonny. Dedicated to Donne, "his one true love, who always encouraged him to be creative and laughed at his jokes and cartoons whether she liked them (or even got them) or not." Faced early with the choice of being a cartoonist or physicist (!), he chose the latter. As Donne writes, "All of his cartoons have the distinction of being rejected by *The New Yorker* magazine."

Sue Geffen: I recommend saving your parents' photos, from which you can create an iPhoto book of their lives that includes a page of their ancestors with dates and names. A written genealogy is important. Letters written to us by co-workers or clients appreciating our talents. Awards or recognition plaques. Trophies for sports. A favorite book. Photos of where we lived with dates and addresses. An address book, eyeglasses, handwritten family recipes, all your business cards, articles you wrote or written about you. An old iphone, portable radio, princess phone, walkman (any old technology). Do not include a list of medicines, pains, and aches!

Leave a Legacy of . . . Interesting

by Phyllis L. Cohen

I'm pretty grateful for the healthy, mostly content people my children have become. I'm not particularly proud of all the life choices made over the years–for example, why did I wait until I purchased my first condo in the New York suburbs before I learned how to drive?

My husband and I seem to have gotten it mostly right with our kids, at least enough of the time to prepare them for the bumps and bruises they will, no doubt, encounter throughout their young adult lives.

How we stay in touch

Now that they're living on their own, we visit with them weekly via FaceTime–a technological Godsend for empty nesters that keeps us connected with our geographically far-flung family. Last summer I started to notice a pattern in our Sunday exchanges with the kids. After we'd chatted about my daughter's recent milestones and accomplishments at her job, and how she was expanding her creative side hustle, our conversation drifted into the silly antics of our dogs and cats. The weekly dialogue with our laconic son, while a bit less breezy, focused on the drama of his uber-demanding consulting job. We would offer him our hard-earned wisdom about how to combat the illusive work-life balance, and I'd share coping strategies on office politics that I'd gleaned from years as one of the working wounded. Sometimes the conversation would drift to finances, or what happened on the latest episode of our shared favorite HBO series. There wasn't much new for me to share about myself, aside from the ever-steady rhythm of a typical week.

Don't get me wrong—all of us look forward to these Sunday night meetups–but I wish I had something more to share with them. It seems that we've left our children with a healthy legacy of thriftiness, a strong ethic of working hard and hopefully the legacy of kindness that it takes to be good citizens of this planet. But I want to leave one more thing—a legacy of living a life that's interesting. Of course, I selfishly want this for myself as well—who doesn't want to live a varied, interesting life? But I want to have an interesting life for the sake of my kids, too.

Little has changed

It took a long time for me to hone my skills as a successful recruiter; a career I've been immersed in since I answered an ad in *The New York Times* after I graduated from college. Over the years the industries I've recruited for have certainly changed, as well as the types of vacancies I've been tasked to fill and the candidates I've engaged in conversation. I've worked from home since my kids were babies—meaning that when I changed jobs over the years, I still sat at the same desk in the same chair in the same home office. The only varying factors were my laptop and a new phone number. My daily commute from bedroom to home office, donning slippers, remained at one solid minute.

It wasn't until about fifteen years ago that I resurrected my childhood passion for writing, starting with writing a couple of novels—a hobby I indulged in so that I'd have something to do in the same room as my kids while they played video games. Of course, I'm writing professionally about a variety of interesting topics these days, and I've devoted time to creating art, spending time with my dogs and immersing myself in nature.

Definitions of "interesting" vary

These days I tell my children about new strides I've made in my writing adventures. I sometimes share incremental advances that I've made in the Autumn of my recruiting career, too. But I'm itching to take more risks—perhaps big ones—so that our Sunday exchanges are inspiring to my children. And I wonder—while I'm responsibly paying the mortgage and helping them repay their college tuition, will there always be interesting stories for me to tell?

Everyone's definition of interesting has its own spin. I've never been an adrenaline junkie—fast cars or extreme sports were never my inclination, even in my twenties. But I still get a rush from the idea of traveling across the country, immersing myself in landscapes different from my own in northeast Pennsylvania. I love meeting new people and figuring out what makes them tick. And if you bring up the possibility of an exotic bird-watching tour in Costa Rica, I'm going to be all ears.

Their needs and mine

When she was four or five years old, I remember how my daughter became upset if I cut my hair drastically or if I wore makeup. She resisted any sudden change I'd make to myself. It made sense to me at the time, since young children crave stability and permanence. They need their parents to stay exactly the same.

Now that I'm creating my own next chapter, I need exactly the opposite.

What do my kids think of this? Despite a few eye rolls or dismissals of ideas that I selectively share about my own reinvention, I'd like to think they're excited for me. I acknowledge that I'm not the center of their lives any more. Yet while my kids are focused, as they should be, on navigating through their own busy professional and personal lives, it is my hope that sharing a few adventures of my own on a Sunday night might seep into their subconscious about how they might look forward to their own middle years one day.

The Boomer generation, including myself as a late entry, is reinventing the idea of retirement (particularly for women) with no frame of reference from any previous generation. While we can never know what our children's lives will look like in middle age, I desperately want to set a good example.

Yes—I admit that it's important for me to lead a somewhat interesting life. Whether I do it for myself, to set an example for my kids or both, I'll never apologize for not being done with figuring out who I want to be, where and how I want to live.

This article by Phyllis L. Cohen originally appeared in BoomerPub. com. She can be reached at LinkedIn.com/in/Phyllis-Cohen-5542b64/.

Reader's Comment

I'm actually planning to write (someday, I hope) about my childhood and early years, before kids and nieces came so that they might know more about my life. I agree, the kids know about how we relate to them and their families, but don't know much about the early me. The conversations are usually about them, and there's not usually time talk about me, except for an occasional anecdote. P.D.

The Circle of Life

by Linda Schwartz

she ushered me into the world
and at the beginning of my life
held me gently in her arms
nurtured and fed me
bathed and dressed me
cleaned up after my accidents
pushed me in a stroller on glorious sunny days
and loved me unconditionally

I ushered her out of this world
and near the end of her life
held her gently in my arms
comforted and fed her
bathed and dressed her
cleaned up after her accidents
pushed her in a wheelchair on glorious sunny days
and loved her unconditionally

parent tending child   child tending parent
within the circle of life

Linda Schwartz is the author of Reflections: Poems about Life, Relationships, and Family.

Acknowledgments

Many thanks to those who helped make the blog on which this book is based a vital community forum. First and foremost, I'd like to recognize the loyal readers of *www.ParentsOfGrownOffspring.com,* who offered valuable suggestions, opinions, and appreciation for the blog's mission. They were at the heart of everything I wrote. Next, I'd like to give a tip of the hat to Cynthia Bert, who designed the warm-looking, yet professional blog and website. I'd also like to recognize John Richardson, my conscientious and knowledgeable SCORE counselor, who not only helped me get the blog off the ground but provided valuable advice in recalibrating it as we went along.

When it comes to thanks, Chris Nolt of Cirrus Book Design, gets a bushelful of it from me. Chris has everything a top creative type should have except the drama. Her skill, patience, and benign aura always make her a joy to work with. On the electronic side, Kathy Moran serves as my never-fail webmaster and Alexandra Trujillo is steadfast in keeping the social media fires burning.

Rounding out the list of those to whom I extend kudos are Betsy Green of the Santa Barbara Independent Writers Group, who is always generous with her time and tips. I'm also indebted to the Santa Barbara Village, Boomer-Life, Antioch University Santa Barbara, and the Federation Women's Division for early invitations to speak.

As to my own adult family, I send big applause for their support, insights and humor. But my appreciation goes above all to my husband, Jon, who, as first reviewer and proofreader, went over every word of every blog. This is a feat worthy not only of thanks but of an Iron Man trophy.

About the Author

Barbara Greenleaf is an accomplished author and speaker who published *www.ParentsOfGrownOffspring.com* for three years. The blog grew out of her interest in the evolution of the family, which can be seen in her earlier books, *Children Through the Ages: A History of Childhood* and *HELP: A Handbook for Working Mothers*, with Lewis A. Schaffer, M.D.

After graduating from Vassar College, Barbara worked at *The Book of Knowledge* and *The New York Times*. She has eight books to her credit, including the award-winning *America Fever: The Story of American Immigration*; *Forward March to Freedom*, a juvenile biography of civil rights leader A. Philip Randolph; and the inspirational young adult novels, *Animal Kingdom* and *Good-to-Go Café*. In addition to her longer works, she has penned numerous articles and speeches, one of which won a Best Speech in L.A. Award and two others that were published in *Vital Speeches of the Day*. She served as a contributing editor at *Working Mother* magazine.

Over the years Barbara applied her communications and consulting skills to the corporate world. She worked for an energy conglomerate and a satellite communications firm before founding Greenleaf Video, a purveyor of nonfiction videos. Later on she started Strategic Communications/LA, where her clients included the RAND Corporation, the Santa Monica Pier, and the SPCA/LA. Most recently, she was Associate Vice Chancellor of Antioch University Santa Barbara.

On the volunteer side, Barbara helped save agricultural land in Goleta, mentored students at Santa Barbara High School, and founded the Santa Barbara Jewish Film Festival. She is married to Jon Greenleaf, with whom she shares two daughters and four grandchildren. When she's not writing, Barbara can be found in her craft room creating mixed media art.

Let's Not Say Goodbye

If you found *Parents of Adult Children: You are Not Alone* to be worthwhile, please leave a review on Amazon. It will encourage other readers to try it.

If you'd like to receive Barbara's free quarterly newsletter, please sign up at *www. barbaragreenleaf.com.*

You can follow Barbara at:

Facebook:
   www.facebook.com/barbaragreenleaf.71
Twitter:
   twitter.com/bkgreenleaf
Instagram:
   www.instagram.com/barbarathewriter/

Made in the USA
Middletown, DE
19 August 2020

15794229R00177